Implementing Recreation and Leisure Opportunities for Infants and Toddlers with Disabilities

Edited by:
Michael Bender
and
Carol Ann Baglin

Sagamore Publishing Inc.
Champaign IL 61820

Book and cover design: Michelle R. Dressen

ISBN: 1-57167-384-9
Library of Congress Catalog Card Number: 2002114448
Printed in the United States.

Sagamore Publishing
804 N. Neil St.
Champaign, IL 61820
www.sagamorepub.com

10 9 8 7 6 5 4 3 2 1

Acknowledgments

It is sometimes difficult to identify those individuals who contribute most to where we are professionally at any one point in our lives. In 1986, when PL 99-457 was enacted, neither of us could have imagined any prospective relationship to early intervention and the Part H, now Part C, system for infants and toddlers with developmental delay and their families. As fate would have it, Carol Ann served as the Director of the Maryland Infants and Toddlers Program in Maryland for eight years, with Michael as the Chairperson of the State Interagency Coordinating Council. This long-term commitment and investment of our energies over these two decades have contributed to us both personally and professionally.

During these years many individuals have been important throughout this process. Carolyn Savage was the administrative assistant, advocate, and ultimately a family specialist in this program from 1988 until 1998 when she unexpectedly passed away. Dr. Nancy S. Grasmick and Senator Barbara Hoffman have been long-time advocates of children, especially those youngest and most vulnerable and their families and both Dr. Grasmick and Senator Hoffman deserve a special thank you. Most of the staff of the Maryland Infants and Toddlers Program from 1988 remain directly involved in the implementation of services at both the state and local level. This kind of commitment over the long haul cannot be measured in years, only through the individual gains of children and their families.

Contents

Foreword

Edward Feinberg, Ph.D.
Program Manager
Anne Arundel County Infants and Toddlers Program
Glen Burnie, Maryland

I am delighted to pay tribute to Michael Bender and Carol Ann Baglin for their excellent work in writing this important book. Drs. Bender and Baglin have reminded us that much of our intervention with infants and toddlers with disabilities can be done through opportunities for play and leisure activities. Too often early intervention is conceptualized as a sequence of therapies that appear to require adults and children to be in a continuous state of work. Children are to work on the development of skills. Adults are to work on encouraging the development of skills. Therapists are to outline the kind of work that must be done by adults and children. In this kind of mindset, it is easy to transform the pleasures of childhood into an endless round of goal-directed activities that are devoid of joy.

Drs. Bender and Baglin challenge us to remember that children with disabilities are children first and that families of children with disabilities are families first. They help us reconsider how, where and when activities can be meaningfully carried out. With the emphasis in Part C of the Individuals with Disabilities Education Act [IDEA] on routines-based intervention in natural environments, they underscore the need to remember that we must figure out creative ways to devise strategies to incorporate developmentally appropriate activities in settings that are enjoyable for children and families. As we move away from a primary emphasis on clinic-based services, clinicians must listen intently to families and learn where particular families spend time and what activities they enjoy pursuing. It is then the obligation of the clinician to assist the family in determining how they can successfully include the child with disabilities in these activities and how these activities can be a source of learning for the child.

The notion of "leisure" is regrettably absent in the vocabulary of many families today. Families are in an eternal state of busy-ness. With dual career couples and working single parents, there is often infrequent opportunity to even contemplate the pursuit of leisure activities. The lives of families of children with disabilities are often a numbing succession of days that feature work, school, and appointments with doctors and therapists. Drs. Bender and Baglin help us figure out ways to carve out time to pursue activities that can be a source of emotional and even spiritual renewal. Trips to the library, the park, the community recreation center, the children's theater, the museum, and the pumpkin patch can be a source of social interaction for parents and children, an opportunity to practice skills that are frequently learned in isolation, and an excursion that can happily include siblings, grandparents and extended family members. And such endeavors can simply be fun!

Dr. Michael Bender and Dr. Carol Ann Baglin have been leaders in the development of early intervention and special education services to children and their families in the state of Maryland. They have also made major contributions to the creation of services throughout the country. This book is a refreshing and practical guide to their belief that the first years of life for children with disabilities and their families are crucial to their longterm development. You will enjoy reading this book and applying its principles to everyday life.

Preface

Audrey N. Leviton L.C.S.W.C.

For the past eighteen years I have been the director of several programs providing services to infants and toddlers with disabilities and their families. This has given me many opportunities to hear families describe the triumphs and challenges of raising a child with special needs. One of the greatest joys frequently mentioned by parents is watching their child experience a life enriched by friends, play, and fun-filled activities. *Recreation and Leisure for Infants and Toddlers with Disabilities* offers parents and caretakers a vision of the rewards that accompany these activities. It is also filled with lots of practical suggestions to turn that vision into a reality.

All children, particularly infants and toddlers, learn most of what they need to know about the world around them through play. Many of the skills necessary in the development of relationships are strengthened through play activities where children are encouraged to communicate, pretend, take turns, etc. Parents of infants and toddlers with disabilities want their children to have these same opportunities. They want their child to have friends who may or may not have disabilities. Parents would like their child to participate in integrated daycare, recreational activities, and play groups. If true integration through recreation and play begins at infancy, the barriers between individuals with disabilities and the rest of society may begin to disappear.

This groundbreaking book offers invaluable ideas for making recreation and leisure an integral part in the lives of infants and toddlers with disabilities. Both families and professionals can learn a wide range of play activities that stimulate cognitive, social, and emotional development. In offering a variety of ideas including such topics as resources, homemade equipment design, curricula ideas, and toy selection, the book addresses the multiple components necessary for the development of comprehensive leisure and recreational program.

A primary theme throughout this book is a respect for the importance of family life. The time families spend together can be greatly enriched by the inclusion of joy, fun, and humor in day-to-day life. This idea is eloquently stated by Holly L. Hatfield-Busk in describing her relationship with her daughter Arian in the article, "A Mother, Not a Therapist."

"What Arian and I were missing was the easy sense of fun for fun's sake. And that is something every child and parent deserves to have. Ten to 20 years from now, I don't want my daughter's only recollections of childhood to be the antiseptic smells of clinical waiting rooms or a dutiful mother who stretched Arian's heelcord the prescribed number of times. We've come to accept these as necessary memories, but I hope they will be accompanied by the rhythm of books and music: the crackle and pungent earthy smell of piles of autumn leaves and the magic of a snowman we built together."

Audrey N. Leviton is Director of Kennedy Krieger Institute's Family Support Services and the child and Family Support Program, a home-based therapy, parent training, and support program for infants and toddlers with disabilities and their families. She is also the executive director of PACT: Helping Children with Special Needs, an affiliate of the Kennedy Krieger Institute. PACT serves infants and toddlers with special needs and their families through programs providing comprehensive assessments, early intervention services, parent education, counseling, and specialized childcare. Ms. Leviton has authored a number of journal articles, produced a prize winning videotape on siblings, and is an editor of the journal, *Infants and Young Children.*

CHAPTER 1
An Overview

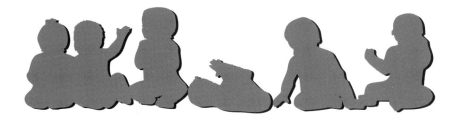

Carol Ann Baglin
Michael Bender

The importance of leisure activities is recognized across all segments of our communities, our states, and this nation. The word "recreation" comes from the Latin "recreare" which means to restore or renew. Each of us finds opportunities through many varieties of sports and leisure activities to express our individuality and refresh our spirits.

Recreation is as important to the disabled in their everyday lives and to their self-esteem as the nondisabled. In fact, for many disabled people, the opportunity for participation in sports is a key to their social and emotional well-being. Like everyone else today, individuals with disabilities have more time to pursue leisure and to socialize with friends. Many are healthier, physically, and able to participate in sports, the arts, and entertainment. With improved access to public facilities, individuals with disabilities can participate in the community, stadiums, parks, and health clubs.

The Special Olympics is an international program of sports training and competition for children and adults with mental retardation. Initially formed in the early 1960s as a day camp for people with mental retardation, the Special Olympics began in 1968 when Eunice Kennedy Shriver organized the First International Special Olympics Games. The Special Olympics oath is "Let me win. But if I cannot win, let me be brave in the attempt." (Special Olympics website). In a salute to the importance of recreation for those with disabilities, Special Olympics promotes physical fitness, motor skills development, improved self-esteem, access to friendships, and increased family involvement.

Federal legislation has been key in securing opportunities for the disabled as a basic civil right. It began in 1954 in *Brown v. Board of Education of Topeka,* which found that the practice of segregated education is illegal and schools must desegregate at "all deliberate speed." At that time any educational programs that existed for the disabled were in special schools and classes for "borderline" and "mildly" retarded—the "educable." The words "mainstream" and "inclusion" had not been applied yet to students with disabilities in their educational setting or environment. The majority of educational programs for students with moderate disabilities were operated by private organizations, e.g., Associations for Retarded Citizens. Children with severe and profound impairments were routinely excluded from any opportunities within the community and were frequently confined to institutions.

The beginning of a change in this pattern of exclusion occurred with the election and inauguration of John F. Kennedy in 1961. In fact, in many respects, the movement for equality for persons with disabilities mirrored the civil rights movement at that time. A new social concern emerged in this time of prosperity for the well-being of all citizens, including those with mental illness and mental retardation. There was an optimism that we could solve all of our problems through federal action. In late 1961 nine months after taking office, JFK established the President's Panel on Mental Retardation with the charge to chart a comprehensive and coordinated attack on the problem of mental retardation. In 1963, Kennedy submitted his historic *Message to Congress Relative to Mental Illness and Mental Retardation* setting the stage for federal involvement in programs and services for persons with disabilities, particularly a call for community-based services. In 1964, President Johnson began building the "Great Society," a key component of which was aiming federal dollars at the education of children from low-income homes. Through improving their educational opportunities, he believed this nation could solve the problems of poverty, delinquency, unemployment, and illiteracy.

The first major involvement of federal government in education came with the passage of P.L. 89-10, The Elementary and Secondary Education Act of 1965 providing grants to state education agencies which were passed on to local school systems to enrich the education provided for children from low-income families. As frequently happens with legislation providing an entitlement for one group, it is expanded to include additional groups. In 1965, there

was an extension of this program for children from economically deprived homes to children with disabilities. The federal involvement in expanding entitlements and funding for the disabled in education has consistently increased to this day.

In a sweeping reform, though still unevenly implemented, the Architectural Barriers Act of 1968 provided for the elimination of architectural barriers to the physically handicapped and stipulated that the construction and renovation of certain buildings had to be accomplished in a manner that made them accessible to persons with physical handicaps. American National Standards Institute (ANSI) issued the first set of accessibility standards in 1961. The standards developed by these agencies, known as the Uniform Federal Accessibility Standards (UFAS), were patterned after the ANSI Standard. Later, upon recognizing that this initial legislative effort was not having its intended effect, Congress established the Architectural and Transportation Barriers Compliance Board. This was done in Section 502 of the Rehabilitation Act of 1973 (PL 93-112).

The mid- and late 1960s were also important because it was then that the plight of our handicapped citizens was brought to public attention. In a landmark decision in 1973 in *Mills v. Board of Education,* the federal district court applied the equal protection clause of the 14th Amendment of the U.S. Constitution to the issue of disability ruling that schools could not discriminate against students on the basis of disability. The 1970s were significant for legislation related to developmental disabilities, e.g., The Developmentally Disabled Assistance and Bill of Rights Act of 1975.

By 1974 Congress was frustrated with the pace of implementation of special education and was confronted with two recent major court decisions, the *Pennsylvania Association for Retarded Citizens (PARC) v. Pennsylvania* (1972) and *Mills v D.C. Board of Education* (1972), both of which made it clear that children with disabilities must be given access to public education (Turnbull & Turnbull, 2000). Congress enacted PL 93-

380, which increased federal aid to special education and required states to adopt a goal of providing full educational opportunities to all children with disabilities. The main purposes were to enforce the 14th amendment and equal protection guarantees on behalf of students with disabilities, help states to carry out duties related to educating all students and assist states to implement state laws, overcoming exclusion of students with disabilities, and reform the school systems to accommodate students with disabilities.

Key developments in recreation legislation also enacted during the period of 1960 to 1980 established programs in rehabilitative services, special education, sports, and recreation. Legislation became an appropriate approach to ensuring access to education, employment, and equal treatment in our society. Following World War II, there had been an expansion of opportunity of the disabled for rehabilitation and vocational services, particularly for veterans. While this period offered limited legislative federal expansion, there was little organized advocacy for special recreation opportunities for the disabled. In addition, there was little state level organization among therapeutic recreation professional. There was some interest in the 1970s with the establishment of a standing committee on Recreation and Leisure within the President's Committee on the employment of the Handicapped (Nesbitt, 1980).

The importance of leisure and recreation opportunities are well known by professionals and others who work with children who have special needs and disabilities. For example, in the area of rehabilitation, the teaching of leisure skills is critical as free time often increases during the rehabilitation process. In a similar manner, young children who are in special education need to learn how to utilize leisure activities and experiences as a prelude to maximizing their non-school hours. Outdoor recreation and sports programs in the community are just beginning to acknowledge the existence of populations of young children with disabilities. The integration of these children into these community experiences has been slow in coming but appears to be moving in a positive direction. Barriers exist in accessing and participating in leisure and recreational opportunities, particularly for the very youngest of our children and their families. While physical barriers predominate, expectations and opportunity are just opening for all persons with disabilities.

Recreation for everyone is accessed through public and private organizations and represents a range of activities from arts and crafts, book clubs, sports, competitive games, and professional teams. This diversity of opportunities presents challenges for change.

The purpose of this book is to enhance and expand the perception of recreation and leisure for young children and their families. With a young child with a disability, the options for leisure activities exist in everyday life, at home, in day care, and within the community.

Chapter Two, **Early Intervention Services for Infants and Toddlers with Disabilities,** provides an overview of the early intervention system for infants and toddlers with disabilities and their families, as required by the Individuals with Disabilities Education Act (IDEA), amended in 1997 as Part C. Specific references are made to types of early intervention services, eligibility, and the national and state perspectives. A discussion of the opportunities for settings for implementation of early intervention is provided, including the home, preschools/nursery schools, child care, Head Start, and the community.

Chapter Three, **Recreation and Leisure for Young Children,** illustrates recreation and leisure as it pertains to young children, with specific reference to infants and toddlers. Included in this discussion are descriptions of the benefits of leisure as well as leisure concepts and settings. A major component of the chapter is a description of curricula ideas for professional and parents, including selecting toys for quality play and activities for infants and toddlers that address their unique needs.

In Chapter Four, *Recreational Opportunities for Families of Young Children with Disabilities,* recreational and leisure activities for families with infants, toddlers, and young children with disabilities, in addition to other family members are addressed, including options available to families, such as appropriate settings. Suggestions are provided and encourage families to take advantage of recreational, social, and leisure opportunities within their community. A major component of the chapter focuses on providing families practical information and options to continue enjoying family activities while including their child with a disability.

Chapter Five, *Recreational or Leisure Activities and the Development of Cognition in Young Children with Disabilities* provides an overview of cognition in young children, while reviewing general principles of supporting cognitive development and applicable strategies for early intervention using opportunities in recreation and leisure. Suggestions for using family recreational activities to facilitate cognitive development are provided.

In an effort to assist in direct application of recreation and leisure activities, Chapter Six, *Adaptive Approaches to Recreation and Leisure Activities for Infants and Toddlers,* examines the unique needs of disabled infants and toddlers and reflects on how these needs impact play skills, use of leisure time, and family needs. Also included in this chapter are curricular implications, strategies and techniques related to developing recreational and leisure skills, use of community facilities and programs, sample activities,

and ideas to promote sibling play. Health professionals are provided with support in Chapter Seven, *Implementing Recreation and Leisure for the Young Child With Health in Mind,* which provides a hands-on approach to implementing early intervention services with specific considerations for health issues. Discussions specific to the full range of options for the provision of early intervention through identified health related services are included.

In Chapter Eight, *Development of Recreation and Leisure Through Art Interventions,* therapeutic art approaches are discussed related to implementing early intervention services. Utilization of art therapy and related interventions and play therapy models with young children can be an effective strategy for providing recreation and leisure and early intervention services. A wide variety of instructional and recreational strategies are reviewed. Finally, Chapter Nine provides a wide range of Resources, including specific books, associations, videos, and internet supports.

References

Nesbitt, J. A. (1980). *A preliminary review of federal legislation for special recreation for disabled in the United States.* Paper presented at the World Congress of Rehabilitation International (14th, Winnipeg, Manitoba, Canada, June 23-27,) 32 pages.

http://.specialolympics.org/about_special_olympics/about_soi.html

Turnbull, H. R., & Turnbull, A. P. (2000). *Free appropriate public education: The law and children with disabilities.* Denver: Love Publishing Co.

CHAPTER 2
Early Intervention Services for Infants and Toddlers with Disabilities

Carol Ann Baglin

Babies need many supports to grow up physically, to develop skills, and to participate in mutual opportunities for nurturing and love within a family. Although babies develop at different paces, some more quickly in one area than another, there are typical stages of growth and development. However, sometimes development may lag sufficiently to heighten concerns for parents, caregivers, and pediatricians. Some babies may need specialized help that exceeds the routine patterns and supports of daily living and parenting skills in order to learn about their world and to master developmentally appropriate tasks. When a family is dealing with the possibility of developmental delay, this can be a difficult time.

Many of these challenging patterns of development can be assisted through early intervention and the provision of specialized services and family supports. Early intervention services are especially critical for new families—those just experiencing the challenges of raising a special family—and is a recognition of the importance of these

early years to the long-term educational outcomes for young children. The hope is that families are assisted, empowered, and supported in their lifetime role as a parent.

Early intervention is a system of services provided to enhance child development and to support the family in acquiring a range of skills to assist their child. Current brain research supports that the first three years are the most critical in acquisition of cognitive and language skills. Early intervention attempts to ameliorate the potential effects of disabilities or risk conditions, such as low birth weight, exposure to lead, drugs, or environmental conditions.

Early intervention services play an important role in knitting together the very significant programs that ensure all children enter school ready to learn and grow to their greatest potential. This program embodies the belief that if the children of today are nurtured as they should be, they can enter school ready to learn and grow to become the healthy, productive adults of tomorrow. By spending relatively few dollars on initiatives of prevention and early intervention for young children and families, we can avoid spending millions as they grow older. Programs designed to intervene early, prevent problems before they occur, and support families are much less expensive and more effective than those that focus on treatment alone.

The inequities in early life experiences require that special efforts be made to ensure that all children have access to these opportunities to promote educational success. Schools in the future must be ready to educate all children—those children with disabilities, at-risk children, children of poverty, non-English speaking, gifted, and talented. In communities across the United States, public agencies and private organizations, professionals and parents, policy makers and everyday citizens are learning creative ways of weaving together, strengthening, and expanding the networks that bring quality services to children and families. Programs of prevention and early intervention are focused on achieving the goal of ensuring that each child has a healthy birth and that each child, during the first five years of life, has all the opportunities and resources necessary to develop fully within a healthy family and be ready to learn.

The changing nature of the family makes service delivery more complex, but early intervention services can be built around the unique needs of each family. The increasing complexity of providing "service" coordination requires a design that supports coordination of the many different services systems for the family. This family-focused model of service delivery can be community based to ensure relevancy to families within their neighborhood communities. As families move into preschool service models, transitioning of the family-centered services becomes an important component of early intervention.

In 1986, there was widespread support to improve access to early intervention and family services for developmentally delayed infants and toddlers and their families, birth to three years old. Congress enacted P. L. 99-457, Part H, reauthorized in 1997 as Part C within the Individuals with Disabilities Education Act (IDEA), to provide early intervention services for infants and toddlers with developmental delays and their families. The overall purposes were to ensure planning and coordination of early intervention services for young children and their families, to provide access and maximize funding, to promote the identification of innovative models related to child development, to enhance the training opportunities for parents and professionals, and to enact policies that would be supportive of early intervention programs.

The Individualized Family Service Plan (IFSP), a fundamental component of Part C, was designed as the primary vehicle for documentation of: (a) a family's resources, concerns, and priorities; (b) early intervention services to ameliorate the effects of a developmental disability; (c) family supports; and (d) identification of an individual to coordinate services for the family. With Part C's innovative approach to services, federal policy related to young children with disabilities shifted from a focus on the child to a focus on (a) the relationship of the child within the family and (b) an interagency service delivery system (Taylor & Baglin, 2000). With the reauthorization of IDEA in 1997, additional opportunities were made available to expand the continuum of early intervention and preschool services for young children with disabilities became a reality. Among the changes to the IDEA, Congress included statutory authority for use of the diagnostic category, developmental delay, for children above the ages of three years to nine years. Developmental delay was previously permitted only for children under three years of age.

Early intervention services include the variety of services that have traditionally been available through special education, as well as certain family-oriented support services. Many states provide early intervention services to infants and toddlers through funding within the local departments of health, social services, and through local education agencies.

A major component of federal policy has been the expressed belief that a comprehensive and coordinated early interven-

CHART 2.1
Early Intervention Services

- Case management
- Audiology
- Physical therapy
- Occupational therapy
- Speech and language pathology
- Family training
- Counseling
- Home visitation

- Health services
- Nursing
- Nutrition counseling
- Assistive technology
- Psychological services
- Social work
- Special instruction
- Transportation
- Others as needed

tion service system, including health and education, will significantly reduce the risk that poor, low-birth weight (LBW), drug affected, and disabled infants will later develop learning problems. Under the requirements of Part C of the Individuals with Disabilities Education Act (IDEA), each state adopts its own definition of developmental delay to determine eligibility and at-risk, if it is to be included in the state's definition. To be considered eligible for early intervention services, an infant or toddler must be experiencing delay in development, manifest atypical development or behavior that is likely to result in subsequent delay, or have a diagnosed physical or mental condition that has a high probability of resulting in developmental delay. Infants and toddlers with high probability conditions are automatically eligible for early intervention services. Federal regulations provide the following examples of diagnoses associated with high probability of developmental delay: Down syndrome and other chromosomal abnormalities, sensory impairment (including vision and hearing), inborn errors of metabolism, microcephaly, severe attachment disorders (including failure to thrive), seizure disorders, and fetal alcohol syndrome. To be considered at-risk for developmental delay, an infant or toddler would show no current abnormality in development but have biologic or environmental factors such as drug exposure or maternal age, that increase the possibility of future developmental delay. Infants and toddlers and their families, determined to be eligible for early intervention services, receive services through the individualized family service plan (IFSP), while those identified as at-risk may be monitored or screened developmentally at specific intervals or provided services determined by each state. The reauthorized Part C encourages the identification of at-risk infants and toddlers and the provision of certain services as an effort to prevent the development of more long-term disabilities.

Each state has the discretion to target services to the at-risk infant and toddler, in addition to the developmentally delayed population. Some states are including some, if not all, of the biologically and environmentally at-risk populations.

The estimated national average for infants and toddlers with developmental delay is approximately 2% of the total birth to 3 population.

Components Of The System

Components of the statewide comprehensive system for the provision of appropriate early intervention services to infants

CHART 2.2

Serving Infants and Toddlers

- Through the coordination of public and private resources,

- Through the development and implementation of a statewide interagency system of early intervention services,

- Single point of entry at the local level,

- Provision of case management for families,

- Development of an individualized family service plan (IFSP) that coordinates resources and services for the family.

and toddlers with specialized needs include a broad range of requirements targeted to the development and implementation of a broad system of state and local supports for infants and toddlers and their families.

The state must provide assurances that it is able to meet the following conditions:
- Services must be provided under **public supervision.**
- Services must be provided **at no cost,** except where federal or state laws allow.
- Services must **be designed to meet the developmental needs** across all areas of delay.
- Services must meet **state standards,** as well as new federal standards.
- Services include, but are not limited to, **family training and counseling, special instruction, speech pathology, occupational therapy, physical therapy, case management, medical evaluation and diagnosis, and screening.**
- Services must be provided by **qualified personnel.**
- Services are delivered in conformity with the **Individualized Family Service Plan (IFSP).**

The **early intervention service delivery** funding for eligible infants and toddlers and their families consists of federal, state, and local funds from specific programs, including those identified within the Act and the implementing regulations:
- Title V of the Social Security Act (Maternal and Child Health)
- Title XIX of the Social Security Act (Medicaid)
- Head Start Act
- Parts B and C of the IDEA
- Subpart 2 of Part D of Chapter 1 of Title I of the Elementary and Secondary Education Act of 1965
- Developmentally Disabled Assistance and Bill of Rights Act
- State and Local funds as related to the provision of early intervention services.

Funding through IDEA, Part C, is provided to states based on a census count of infants and toddlers, birth to three years of age. Other funding is distributed based on certain eligibility requirements for each of the programs specific to individual children.

Why Provide Early Intervention Services

Infants and toddlers, even those perceived as developing normally but identified at an early age as high-risk or those with developmental delay, are at a greater

CHART 2.3

Components of the Early Intervention System

- State **definition of "developmentally delayed"** and assurances of consistent application in local jurisdictions;
- Comprehensive **multidisciplinary evaluation** of the needs of the infants and their families;
- Development of an **individualized family service plan (IFSP)** for each eligible infant and toddler and his/her family;
- Provision of **case management services** for the interagency delivery of services;
- **Interagency outreach** child find and referral system through a **single point of entry at the local level;**
- **Public awareness plans** at the state and local level;
- **Central directory of early intervention services** and resources, experts, research, and demonstration projects;
- Single line of authority in a **state lead agency,** for:
  - administration and supervision
  - identification and coordination of all available resources
  - assignment of financial responsibility to the appropriate agency
  - procedures to ensure the provision of service and to resolve intra- and interagency disputes
  - entry into formal interagency agreements
- Development of **policies** for contracting or making arrangements with local service providers and the timely reimbursement of funds;
- System of **procedural safeguards;**
- Policies and procedures for **personnel standards;**
- System of **interagency data collection** for the early intervention programs.

risk than their peers for learning or behavior problems during the primary elementary grades. An analysis of the literature indicates a wide range of strategies have been implemented to address the needs of young children with certain types of risk factors and developmental delays. The research related to the implementation of traditional models for infant and toddler services delivery produces weak effects, with few studies showing developmental improvement, particularly with the more traditional models of home delivery (Halpern, 1984; LeLaurin, 1992). The level of intervention may be too little since most children are awake nearly 4,000 hours yet only receive about 1% of these hours of early intervention services. Research results (LeLaurin, 1992; Guralnick, 1988) are variable, indicating a need to reassess these strategies of intervention and to expand what may be considered early intervention services. Any one model for all children may not meet the needs of some with or without developmental delay. Developmental, functional, and biological models were examined (Mallory, 1992). The developmental model fostered play, discovery, problem solving, and practice. Functional independence was seen as a means toward social acceptance and value. Developmentally appropriate practice, advocated by the National Association for the Education of Young Children (NAEYC), focuses on age and individual appropriateness of learning experiences, allowing the child to make choices about what is learned (Lowenthal, 1992).

The family-focused intervention model was implemented with families having infants with moderate or severe disabilities (Caro & Derevensky, 1991). Parents perceived significant progress in the ability of their families to meet the challenges of caring for young children with disabilities. Fewell & Oelwein (1991) studied the effectiveness of an intervention program for young children enrolled in outreach sites of a program for children with Down Syndrome and other developmental delays. The rate of development during intervention was higher compared to the rate of development at the pretest period. Ramey & Ramey (1992) summarized findings related to the prevention of mental retardation in children of low-IQ mothers at risk of poor outcomes. The positive outcomes of early intervention in the first five years of life lasted until early adolescence. Early intervention is associated with an almost 50% reduction in the rate of failing a grade, and a reduction in borderline functioning from 44% for the control group to 13% for children receiving intervention. These works support the efficacy of early intervention with at-risk infants and toddlers and the long-term benefits.

Through information obtained from the U.S. Census Bureau's Survey of Income and Program Participation (SIPP), estimates suggest that there were as many as 851,000 children with disabilities during the 1991-92 school year. Approximately 80% of these children were estimated to have received developmental services (Bowe, 1995). There is some evidence with regard to the cost effectiveness of early intervention for at-risk populations compared with intervention for children with disabilities (Escobar, Barnett, & Goetze, 1994; Warfield, 1995). The factors that were found to have the greatest impact on cost were program duration and frequency (measured in hours per year, intensity of services, (staff-child ratio), geographic location, and contributed resources. The least expensive programs were those providing a high number of service hours in a center-based setting serving preschoolers. The highest costs per hour were in home-based programs. Several factors contributed to making programs either expensive or inexpensive, including number of children, the amount of service provided, and staff-child ratio. The younger children were more likely to make positive gains per hours on measures of outcome. The largest change per hour values were associated with group services for young children (Warfield, 1995).

Children with disabilities such as mild mental retardation, learning disabilities, and behavior problems were not usually identified until they encountered school problems, particularly between the ages of 8 and 12 years. Other children who are medically high-risk are usually identified in their primary school years (Harel & Anastasiow, 1985). These children are at developmental risk due to certain characteristics of their birth or environmental experience. Research has established a statistically reliable link between low birthweight (LBW) and disabling conditions, but has not quantified the risk of educational disabilities among these medically high-risk children compared to their normal birthweight (NBW) peers (Carran, et al, 1989). The study compared the relative risk of educational exceptionalities for very low birthweight (VLBW) (birthweight less than 1,500 grams) and low birthweight (birthweight 1,500 to 2,500 grams) to normal birthweight (greater than 2,500 grams) group. The study was conducted on two birth cohorts to determine if relative risk varies by age. The results showed no significant differences between cohorts for the medical variables of birthweight, gestational age (GA), head circumference, or birth length. Significant mean differences within cohorts and among birthweight groups for all of these variables were found. All of the severe conditions were found in the LBW and VLBW of Cohort II and the VLBW of Cohort I. The combined risk ratio for VLBW and LBW to experience educational problems was determined to be 1.93 times that for NBW children. In addition, the study found that infants from low-income homes who are between 1,500 and 2,500 grams are at very elevated risk for mild educational disabilities than normal peers.

Research (Fewell & Glick, 1996; Schraeder, 1993) on intensive early intervention programs revealed that in cognition, gross motor, and fine motor skills, the groups with less severe impairments make more progress. Nurses in schools are frequently asked about the school problems of children born with VLBW. Many VLBW children do have special learning needs and so score lower than the NBW. The studies in this area routinely support the importance of detecting academic risk early (Schnudtm & Wedig, 1990). Based on the results of numerous studies, the Institute of Medicine cited low birth weight as a major determinant of infant mortality (Abel, 1997). LBW is a biosocial risk resulting from a combination of biological factors such as medical risk during pregnancy and social factors such as poverty and maternal stress. Six to seven percent of all infants born in the U.S. are of low birth weight (Kopp & Kaler, 1989).

There is a paucity of research on the long-term outcomes of children exposed to a wide range of drugs. Differential intervention efforts based primarily on knowledge of a child's intrauterine exposure to drugs was unsupported by research. National estimates of drug use by women who are pregnant are not readily available. A summary of the literature (Shriver & Piersel, 1994) on the long-term physiological effects of intrauterine drug exposure for child development concluded that except for children diagnosed with Fetal Alcohol Syndrome, it is not possible to predict the outcomes for individual children exposed prenatally to drugs. Intervention based on current knowledge is not supported. The authors recommend research into how child physiological variables (i.e. prenatal drug exposure) and environmental variables (e.g., parent management skills) interact so that all children and their families can receive the most effective early childhood services. It would appear that we know more about the immediate impact following birth rather than long-term implications for children in the preschool and primary years.

Effectiveness Of Early Intervention

The effectiveness of early intervention programs for children with developmental disabilities and for children at biologic risk (Guralnick, 1991) indicated a significant pattern of improvement in developmental milestones. The ability of early intervention programs to minimize declines in development appears to be the most significant outcome (Arcia, Keyes, Gallagher, & Herrick, 1993). Stresses (Baxter & Kahn 1996) include food, shelter, transportation, medical, informal and personal time needs. Developmental outcome can be understood only through joint consideration of organismic, environmental, and interactional factors (LeLaurin, 1992). Horowitz (1985) suggested that a continuously facilitative environment is the optimum for development. Some children are more vulnerable, with a higher risk possibility for risk, particularly where organismic vulnerability is present. Children who began intervention earliest and where there was direct intervention with the families, so that the parents became the child's primary interventionists, had the most positive results, with children making the greatest gains.

State policy has important implications for decisions around who gets intervention, what types of services are included, and how to allocate funds to children with less severe deficits (Fewell & Glick, 1996; McCormick, Gortmaker, & Sobol, 1990). It is hoped that a sufficient number of children with developmental concerns and those with a combination of risk factors can be identified in the primary school years. The literature supports that it is these children who, if provided early intervention services, would make the most significant developmental gains and would also be a cost-effective investment in the prevention of more serious educational problems in later years.

Accessing Early Intervention

While Part C of the Individuals with Disabilities Education Act was enacted to assist states to enhance the capacity of families to meet the specialized needs of their infants and toddlers with disabilities, the child is the focus of services and eligibility.

The law is the framework to provide early intervention services to eligible infants and toddlers through the individualized family services plan (IFSP). The individualized family service plan is based on principles originally identified by NEC*TAS/ACCH (1989).

The IFSP is developed to provide a written document of the interagency, collaborative efforts to document those resources and services that are identified to meet the developmental needs of families and eligible infants and toddlers.

Parents, physicians, and caregivers may have a concern related to the development of an infant or toddler. A referral is made to a single point of entry that initiates a process of evaluation and assessment that must be completed within 45 days. A service coordinator assists the family throughout this process and coordinates the development of the IFSP for eligible infants and toddlers. Many infants, identified at a very young age, may have extensive information that is helpful to this process and will inform the decisions that are made by the family and professionals. Through this process families identify needs and resources which will support their role with their child. Many families find the terms used throughout this process to be confusing, but an understanding is important to the qual-

---

CHART 2.4

Principles

Infants and toddlers are uniquely dependent on their families for their survival and nurturance. This dependence necessitates a family-centered approach to early intervention.

States and programs should define "family" in a way that reflects the diversity of family patterns and structures.

Each family has its own structure, roles, values, beliefs, and copying styles. Respect for and acceptance of this diversity is a cornerstone of family-centered early intervention.

Respecting family autonomy, independence, and decision making means that families must be able to choose the level and nature of early intervention's involvement in their life.

Family/professional collaboration and partnerships are the keys to family-centered early intervention and to successful implementation of the IFSP process.

An enabling approach to working with families requires that professionals re-examine their traditional roles and practices and develop new practices when necessary — practices that promote mutual respect and partnerships.

Early intervention services should be flexible, accessible, and responsive to family needs.

Early intervention services should be provided according to the normalization principle—that is, families should have access to services provided in as normal a fashion and environment as is possible and that promote the integration of the child and family within the community.

No one agency or discipline can meet the diverse and complex needs of infants and toddlers with special needs and their families. Therefore, a team approach to planning and implementing the IFSP is necessary.

Set forth in *Guidelines and Recommended Practices for the Individualized Family Service Plan* (NEC*TAS/ACCH, 1989):

CHART 2.5

Glossary

Assessment means the ongoing procedures used by appropriate qualified personnel throughout the period of a child's eligibility to identify (a) the child's unique strengths and needs and the services appropriate to meet those needs; and (b) the resources, priorities, and concerns of the family, and the supports and services necessary to enhance the family's capacity to meet the developmental needs of the child.

Early intervention services means services which are (a) designed to meet the developmental needs of the eligible child and the needs of the family related to enhancing the child's development; (b) selected in collaboration with the parents; (c) provided under public supervision, by qualified personnel, in conformity with an individualized family service plan, and at no cost to families, unless federal or State law provides for a system of payments by families, including sliding fees; (d) consistent with the standards of the State; and (e) to the maximum extent appropriate to the needs of the child, provided in natural environments, including the home and community settings in which children without disabilities participate.

Evaluation means the procedures used by appropriate qualified personnel to determine a child's initial and continuing eligibility, consistent with the definition of infants and toddlers with disabilities, including determining the status of the child in each of the following developmental areas: (a) cognitive development; (b) physical development, including vision and hearing; (c) communication development; (d) social or emotional development; and (e) adaptive development.

Individualized Family Service Plan (IFSP) means a written plan for providing early intervention and other services to an eligible child and the child's family, which shall: (a) be developed jointly by the family and appropriate qualified personnel involved in the provision of early intervention services; (b) be based on the multidisciplinary evaluation and assessment of the child, and the assessment of the child's family; and (c) include services necessary to enhance the development of the child and the capacity of the family to meet the special needs of the child.

Infants and toddlers with disabilities (sample State definition) means children from birth through 2 years old who are eligible for early intervention services, as documented by appropriate qualified personnel, because they: (a) are experiencing at least a 25% delay, as measured and verified by appropriate diagnostic instruments and procedures, in one or more the following developmental areas (cognitive development, physical development [including vision and hearing], communication development, social or emotional development, or adaptive development); or (b) manifest atypical development or behavior, which is demonstrated by abnormal quality of performance and function in one or more of the above specified developmental areas, interferes with current development, and is likely to result in subsequent delay, even when diagnostic instruments or procedures do not document a 25% delay; or (c) have a diagnosed physical or mental condition that has a high probability of resulting in developmental delay, with examples of these conditions including chromosomal abnormalities, genetic or

CHART 2.5

Glossary (continued)

congenital disorders, severe sensory impairments, inborn errors of metabolism, disorders reflecting disturbance of the development of the nervous system, congenital infections, disorders secondary to exposure to toxic substances, including fetal alcohol syndrome, and severe attachment disorders.

Interim service coordinator means the individual designated at the single point of entry to assist the referred child and the child's family through the initial multidisciplinary evaluation and assessment and individualized family service plan process.

Multidisciplinary means the involvement of two or more disciplines or professions in the provision of integrated and coordinated services, including evaluation and assessment activities and the development of the IFSP.

Natural environments means settings that are natural or normal for the child's age peers who have no disability.

Parent means a parent, a guardian, a person acting as a parent of a child, or a surrogate parent who has been appointed in accordance with established procedures.

Qualified personnel means persons who have met State approved or recognized certification, licensing, registration, or other comparable requirements that apply to the area in which the personnel are providing early intervention services.

Qualified personnel who provide early intervention services are responsible for: (a) consulting with parents, other service providers, and representatives of appropriate community agencies to ensure the effective provision of services in the area in which they provide service; (b) training parents and others regarding the provision of those services; (c) participating in the multidisciplinary team's assessment of a child and the child's family, and in the development of integrated goals and outcomes for the individualized family service plan.

Service coordination means the activities carried out by a service coordinator to assist and enable an eligible child and the child's family to receive the rights, procedural safeguards, and services that are authorized to be provided under the State's early intervention system. Each eligible child and the child's family must be provided with one service coordinator who is responsible for (a) coordinating all services across agency lines and (b) serving as the single point of contact in helping parents to obtain the services and assistance they need.

Service coordination is an active process that involves: (a) assisting parents of eligible children in gaining access to the early intervention services and other services identified in the individualized family service plan; (b) coordinating the provision of early intervention services and other services (such as medical services for other than diagnostic and evaluation purposes) that the child needs or is being provided; (c) facilitating the timely delivery of available services; and (d) continuously seeking the appropriate services and situations necessary to benefit the development of each

CHART 2.5
Glossary (continued)

child being served for the duration of the child's eligibility.

Service coordination activities include: (a) coordinating the performance of evaluations and assessments; (b) facilitating and participating in the development, review, and evaluation of individualized family service plans; (c) assisting families in identifying available service providers; (d) coordinating and monitoring the delivery of available services; (e) informing families of the availability of advocacy services; (f) coordinating with medical and health providers; and (g) facilitating the development of a transition plan to preschool services, if appropriate.

Service coordinator means the individual designated in the individualized family service plan to carry out service coordination activities. Service coordinators may be employed or assigned in any way that is permitted under State law, so long as it is consistent with Part C requirements. A State's policies and procedures for implementing the statewide system of early intervention services must be designed and implemented to ensure that service coordinators are able to effectively carry out on an interagency basis the functions and services listed above.

Service coordinators must have demonstrated knowledge and understanding about: (a) eligible children; (b) Part C of IDEA and 34 CFR 303; and (c) the nature, scope, and availability of services within the early intervention system, the system of payments for early intervention services, and other pertinent information.

The above terms are taken from the Maryland Individualized Family Service Plan Process and are included for quick reference.

ity of services and supports, as well as empowering the family to act as an advocate on behalf of their child.

The Role of Play in Early Intervention

Play is primarily a mode of learning for young children. It affords parents and early intervention providers with a wide array of strategies to interact and teach the young child. The relationship of play and leisure activities to the development of young children will be more thoroughly explored in later chapters. The role of play in the development of skills is the foundation of intervention for infants and toddlers. There are many studies that identify play as significant to language production and the development of communication skills for very young children. Many professionals rely on play to implement transdiciplinary assessment models.

Play can be used to assess skills, to support development, and to assist in the utilization of play behaviors to support the parent-child relationship. Play can be used to assess specific developmental domains, including communication, physical development, social skills, and cognition while providing opportunities for recreation and leisure. Play is a mechanism to help parents by providing an opportunity to spend more time with their infants and toddlers.

Play is fundamental to developmentally appropriate practices that will develop the competencies young children need to enter school ready to learn. This approach

Chart 2.6

BENEFITS

- Early childhood education can assist Maryland in reaching the educational goal of ensuring that each child is ready to learn;
- Investment in early intervention can reduce costs later by decreasing the impact of developmental disabilities and cut the demand for special education by one third;
- Support services to families with developmentally disabled children preserves the family and enhances their parenting skills;
- Coordination of services can reduce duplication of services and maximize the shrinking human service dollar;
- Case Management links the family with all available services ensuring a comprehensive approach to the family's needs.

is of greater significance with young children with developmental disabilities that need early life experiences to develop their potential within a nurturing and inclusive environment.

Natural environments are the places and routines in which infants and toddlers typically live, learn, and play as described in Appendix A. When early intervention takes place in the home, child care center, or other places where children spend their time, and is made part of the child's and family's routines, infants and toddlers with disabilities learn and practice developmental skills supported by their families and caregivers.

In the literature, play has been characterized as a "developmental concept" that can be used to assess the sequential nature of skill acquisition (Fewell, Ogura, Notari-Syverson & Wheeden, 1997; Fewell & Kaminski, 1988). A wide range of materials can be selected to enhance and support this process, particularly when young children with developmental challenges are included with normally developmenting skills.

The process of leisure and play for young children is the main context that skill development may take place. Everyone is comfortable with interactions which are based on games, songs, or simple physical activities. With young children with disabilities, these "normal" activities may need to be adapted for cognitive or physical developmental challenges. Frequently, parents may need support to acquire the skill to both play and teach. Professionals from the many disciplines providing developmental interventions may also need supports in identifying options within play to intervene effectively. Many professionals may be "experts" in their fields while unfamiliar with the unique aspects of infants and toddlers and their developmental needs.

Cooperative play for young children with disabilities is enhanced through the availability of toys that enhance language development and social skills. Play can provide opportunities for the caregiver and teacher to structure learning opportunities to improve development and solicit social learning. Inclusion with young children with disabilities can be facilitated through improved access to toys that increase interactions (Martin, Brady, & Williams, 1991).

Play made be used to provide sequencing opportunities for the development of skills that are emerging through the process of early intervention. Frequently, the options may need to be systematically integrated into early intervention, however natural the process of play. It is hoped that professionals and families will be provided information and creative supports to implement early intervention and learn the joys of leisure and play as an important setting for learning.

References

Abel, M. H. (1997). Low birth weight and interactions between traditional risk factors. *Journal of Genetic Psychology, 158,* p. 443-454.

Arcia, E., Keyes, L., Gallagher, J., & Herrick, H. (1993). National portrait of socio-demographic factors associated with underutilization of services: relevance to early intervention. *Journal of Early Intervention, 17*(3), 283-297.

Baxter, A., & Kahn, J. V. (1996). Effective early intervention for inner-city infants and toddlers: Assessing social supports, needs, and stress. *Infant Toddler Intervention: The Transdisciplinary Journal, 6*(3), 197-211.

Bowe, F. G. (1995). Population estimates: Birth-to-5 children with disabilities. *The Journal of Special Education, 28*(4), 461-471.

Caro, P., & Derevensky, J. L. (1991). Family-focused intervention model: Implementation and research findings. *Topics in Early Childhood Special Education, 11*(3), 66-80.

Carran, D. T., Scott, K. G., Shaw, K., & Beydouin, S. (1989). The relative risk of educational handicaps in two birth cohorts of normal and low birth weight disadvantaged children. *Topics in Early Childhood Special Education. 9*(1), 14-31.

Escobar, C. M., Barnett, W. S., & Goetze, L. D. (1994). Cost analysis in early intervention. *Journal of Early Intervention 18*(1), 48-63

Fewell, R. R., & Glick, M P. (1996). Program evaluation findings of an intensive early intervention program. *American Journal on Mental Retardation, 101*(3), 233-243.

Fewell, R. R., & Kaminski, R. (1988). Play skills development and instruction for young children with handicaps. In S. L. Odom & M. B. Karnes (Eds.), *Early intervention for infants and children with handicaps* (pp. 145-158). Baltimore: Brookes.

Fewell, R. R., & Oelwein, P. L. (1991). Effective early intervention: Results from the model preschool program for children with Down Syndrome and other developmental delays. *Topics in Early Childhood Special Education, 11*(1), 56-68.

Fewell, R. R., Ogura, T., Notari-Syverson, A. & Wheeden, C. A., (1997). The relationship between play and communication skills in young children with Down Syndrome. *Topics in Early Childhood Special Education, 17*(1), pp. 303-318.

Guralnick, M. J. (1988). Efficacy research in early childhood intervention programs. In S. L. Odom, & M. B. Iarnes (Eds.). *Early intervention for infants & children with handicaps: An empirical base* (pp. 75-88). Baltimore: Brookes.

Guralnick, M. J. (1991). The next decade of research on the effectiveness of early intervention. *Exceptional Children, 58*(2), 174,183.

Halpern, R. (1984). Lack of effects of home-based early intervention? Some possible explanations. *American Journal of Orthopsychiatry, 54,* 33-42.

Harel, S., & Anastasiow, N. J. (Eds.), (1985). *The at-risk infant: Psycho/Socio/ Medical aspects.* Baltimore: Paul H. Brookes.

Horowitz, F. D. (1985). Making a model of development and its implications for working with young infants. *Zero to Three, 6*(2), 1-6.

Kopp, C. B., & Kaler, S. R. (1989). Risk in infancy. *American Psychologist, 44,* 224-230.

LeLaurin, K. (1992). Infant and toddler models of service delivery: Are they detrimental for some children and families? *Topics in Early Childhood Special Education, 12*(1), 82-104.

Lowenthal, B. (1992). Functional and developmental models: A winning early intervention combination. *Infant-Toddler Intervention: The Transdisciplinary Journal, 2*(3), 161-168.

Mallory, B. L. (1992). Is it always appropriate to be developmental? Convergent models for early intervention practice. *Topics in Early Childhood Special Education, 11*(4), 1-12.

Martin, S., Brady, M., & Williams, R. (1991). Effects of toys on the social behavior of preschool children in integrated and nonintegrated groups: Investigation of setting event. *Journal of Early Intervention, 15,* 153-161.

Maryland Infants and Toddlers Program. (1999). *Dreams & challenges: A family's guide to the Maryland Infants & Toddlers Program.* Baltimore.

McCormick, M. D., Gortmaker, S. L., & Sobol, A. M. (1990). Very low birth weight children: Behavior problems and school difficulty in a national sample. *The Journal of Pediatrics, 117,* 687-693.

NEC*TAS/ACCH (1989). *Guidelines and recommended practices for the individualized family service plan.* U.S. Department of Education: Washington, D.C.

Ramey, C. T., & Ramey, S. L. (1992). Effective early intervention. *Mental Retardation, 30*(6), 337-345.

Schraeder, B. D. (1993). Assessment of measures to detect preschool academic risk in very low birth weight children. *Nursing Research, 42,* 17-21.

Schnudtm R. E., & Wedig, K. E. (1990). Very low birth weight infants-Education outcome at school age from parental questionnaire. *Clinical Pediatrics, 29*(11), 649-651.

Shriver, M. D., & Piersel, W. (1994). The long-term effects of intrauterine drug exposure: Review of recent research and implications. *Topics in Early Childhood Special Education, 14*(2), 161-83.

Taylor, J. M., & Baglin, C. A. (2000). Families of young children with disabilities: Perceptions in the early childhood special education literature. *Infant-Toddler Intervention: The Transdisciplinary Journal, 10*(4), 239-257.

Warfield, M. E. (1995). The cost-effectiveness of home visiting versus group services in early intervention. *Journal of Early Intervention, 19*(2), 130-148.

CHAPTER 3
Recreation and Leisure for Young Children

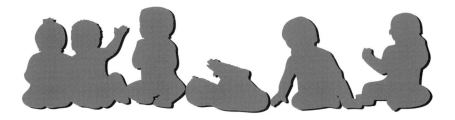

Michael Bender
Carol Ann Baglin

With the renewed interest in improving the quality of life for all persons, leisure, play, and recreational activities have become an important life goal for all ages of individuals. This is especially true for young children with disabilities who often require more individualization and direct learning experiences. There is a growing awareness that leisure, which can be defined as what one does during his or her free time, transcends age boundaries. It is equally valuable as an area of instruction for those who are teaching individuals advancing in age as much as for those teaching infant, toddler, and preschool children. Historically, leisure activities were globally defined and placed under the training domain of a variety of professionals, including occupational therapists, physical educators, therapeutic recreation specialists, and special educators. Leisure and recreation were often viewed as sports-related, competitive activities that were secondary to more basic curricular areas. For many individuals with disabilities, recreation activities and their related experiences have been nonexistent or difficult to access. When programs did emphasize leisure education, they typically were provided by parks and recreation agencies or by specialists working in the areas of recreation, therapeutic recreation, and physical education. There has been little or no strategic planning for the inclusion of leisure and recreational experiences in the everyday lives of individuals with disabilities with their non-disabled peers. It has only been recently that leisure is viewed as a way of enhancing the development or socialization, mobility, independence, and community integration of these individuals. (Bender, Valletutti, & Baglin, 1998).

Many children with disabilities participate in segregated environments for recreation and leisure activities. When given an opportunity for more inclusive settings, these same children will readily participate in the activities more fully with their nondisabled peers. Children with disabilities, like others in this 21st century, have more time to be physically active and socially and physically healthier.

Advances in recreation have provided access to all individuals with disabilities. While accessibility issues are crucial to opportunity, instruction and adaptation of equipment contribute to the challenges facing young children with disabilities. With assistance, young children with disabilities can establish relationships, skills, and increased play repertoires similar to typically developing children.

With the current and growing knowledge of the importance of leisure, other disciplines have begun to seek out leisure curricula. For example, professionals working in the area of psychology as behavior interventionists are now integrating leisure activities into their own protocols. This provides them the opportunity to teach life skills such as risk taking, socialization, and problem solving within a context of everyday leisure and life experiences.

Leisure, in a comprehensive educational context, offers an innovative channel that:

1. Allows an individual to know himself in relation to others.
2. Enhances the quality of his life.
3. Addresses his specific needs, capabilities, and values through the self-selection of meaningful experiences.
4. Enables an individual to evaluate his use of time and behaviors in situations ranging from the simple to complex.
5. Teaches critical social and interpersonal skills (Mathews, 1977).

Leisure as Part of Home Life

When leisure activities are not well thought out and routinely forced upon children, their potential for positive short-or long-term benefits often diminishes. A good example is when parents provide an activity of leisure they themselves like without considering the possible interests of their child. If the activity is not age appropriate, relevant, or appealing, the chances of the child wanting to repeat the activity are not very good.

Play with one's peers and participating in a wide range of planned recreational activities are central to young children's growth and development. Many children with disabilities have fewer opportunities within their communities to participate with their families in play and recreation to develop those skills important to socialization and physical fitness. These children and their families require interventions that encourage and focus leisure (Johnson, Bullock, & Ashton-Shaeffer, 1997). Children involved in leisure activities are provided opportunities to develop friendships, explore interests, and learn specific skills which are applicable in a wide range of settings. The involvement of families leads to family bonding and contextual memories that become an important component of the family unit.

While the child may actively repeat the activity once or twice, it most likely will not become part of their repertoire once they begin to independently choose their leisure experiences. That is why it is important to provide an array of experiences within the home, as well as other places as part of an overall leisure program. Some of these activities will end up being preferred ones while others will not. For example, teaching a young child to complete a puzzle is an excellent activity as it can provide experiences in problem solving, doing independent work, and can utilize an array of fine motor skills. However, if the puzzle is one in which the child has no interest, or is above or below his ability level, causing frustration or boredom, it will serve little purpose in promoting lifelong leisure activities. In fact, puzzles as a taxonomy category under board games, if not presented thoughtfully, may create a negative experience, leading to avoidance of future involvement in this leisure area. That is why leisure activities at all levels, including infants and toddlers, should be well thought out before they are presented as part of a routine experience.

Leisure in the School

Methodology and approaches to teaching the area of leisure have either been narrowly defined or absent altogether from educational programs. In part, this is often because of the widely held belief of many professionals and parents that leisure activities are of secondary importance in planning programs of instruction. More recently, leisure is becoming more broadly defined through activities that facilitate relaxation, fun, amusement, (Moon, 1994), and adventures (Havens, 1992). Bedeni, Bullock, and Driscoll (1993) presented the need for school programs to teach leisure education so individuals with disabilities will know how to "enjoy and use their leisure" (p.72).

Leisure opportunities for young children with disabilities provide numerous avenues for the development of cognitive skills, social and interpersonal skills, physical development, motor and perceptual skills, and the development of positive behaviors. Perhaps the most important reason to develop leisure skills for children with disabilities at a young age is the eventual need for these skills when they grow older. We now know that many older individuals with disabilities have disproportionate amounts of free time due to the difficulty they have in finding or retaining jobs, being unemployed or underemployed, or for medical reasons that restrict their number of work hours.

Educational curricula usually focus on the training of special education and adaptive physical education teachers on techniques and methods to assist young children to learn age-appropriate skills. In addition, the selection of materials that are age-appropriate and can be manipulated by children with disabilities is important in the educational setting. Instructional methodology can be used to teach play skills in the educational context and build interpersonal skills. As much of the equipment and materials are not designed for use with children with significant disabilities, adaptations in design and implementation must be effected to be useful in the educational setting.

Leisure in the Community

The right to participate in leisure pursuits, especially those activities and events that utilize community resources, has often been difficult for individuals with disabilities. Even with a community's increasing awareness of the Americans with Disabilities Act, most families of individuals with disabilities have to actively pursue resources for their children that are easily available for other families. While there has been improved accessibility and community integration for individuals with disabilities, this has often been the result of diligent work of advocacy groups or political assistance from others. As young children with disabilities grow up, they and their families have become more and more militant in asking or demanding for leisure rights and opportunities that are routinely available to the non-disabled community.

Leisure experiences are a positive and valuable resource to people as they function on a daily basis in society (Bender, 1994: Wehman & Schleien, 1980). Leisure experiences facilitate learning, adapting, and adjusting during non-work hours; combat negative stress (Compton & Iso-Ahola, 1994); develop physical fitness; and foster relaxation.

With increasing emphasis on inclusion in school programs and community events, there will be an increasing need to expose young children to a wide range of recreational and leisure activities. These activities offer new ways to interact with peers and others in settings that are less artificial, and more authentic and contextual.

Adequate planning with community members is needed so they will begin to see that young children learn quickly and can be integrated into many situations that previously have provided children with limited exposure.

Leisure Materials and Selection

There are numerous ways to explore the availability of appropriate materials used for leisure activities. For example, one can review information by *Subject Content,* by *Theme,* and by *Parent and Teacher/Professional Recommendations.* Much of this information is now in catalog form and can be easily found on the Internet. It is best to use search engines to find specific types of materials or areas, as specific internet sites and addresses appear to change on a regular basis. Well-known toy stores and educational publishers will be glad to send you their latest material and information via fax or mail if you prefer. Listed below are some ideas for consideration:

Toddlers

There is a full spectrum of *subject content* available for toddler leisure activities. Most toy and educational companies have developed an Early Learning section to go along with traditional sections addressing reading and writing areas. Many companies have also organized their products to address the specific needs of children with disabilities. The math and science areas, have also grown in importance as evidenced by the increase in the amount of board and strategy games and the hands-on science activities being presented for younger audiences.

Themes continue to constitute a comprehensive way of providing a variety of leisure activities. Examples of themes can include: shapes and colors, types of music, letters and numbers, wildlife, temperature and senses, and holidays and heroes. *Parents and Teachers* also have their favorite leisure activities, many of which include commercial games and toys as well as home-made materials.

The examples below* are a *partial* idea of what is available and currently being purchased by parents and other consumers that have worked well with children with special needs. In some instances, a toy or game may have to be adapted, but overall the items presented below fit age-appropriate and educational criteria for promoting positive leisure activities and experiences.

*(Source: SmarterKids.com)

Toddlers

- The Little Hands Art Book
- JumpStart Toddlers
- Aquarium Shape Sorter
- Musical Marble Run
- Mr. Potato Head Says
- Dr. Seuss Reading Games
- Where is Thumbkin? (cassette)
- Tap 'n Turn Bench
- Feltkids Interactive Storybooks
- Tin Drum
- Raffi-Singable Songs for the Very Young (CD)
- Sesame Street Smart Sounds Safari
- Teletubbies Like to Dance
- Nature Campsite (plastic)
- Playing Poohsticks (board book)
- Dr. Seuss Reading (story books)
- Arthur's Reading Games
- Storytime Finger Puppets

Preschool and Kindergarten

- Play Along with Whimzie
- Madeline Classroom Companion: Preschool & Kindergarten
- Elmo's Art Workshop
- Millie and Bailey's Preschool
- Little Bear Thinking Adventure Kindergarten
- Alphabet elephant
- The M&M's Counting Book
- Kids on Stage
- Clapping & Tapping from Bach to Rock
- Sesame Street Pirate Ship
- The Original Colorforms Set
- View Master Dinosaurs

References

Bedeni, L. A., Bullock, C. C., & Driscoll, B. (1993, Second quarter). The effects of leisure education on factors contributing to the successful transition of students with mental retardation from school to adult life. *Therapeutic Recreation Journal,* pp. 70-82.

Bender, M. (1994). Learning disabilities: Beyond the school years. In A. Capute, P. Accardo, & B. Shapiro (Eds.), *Learning disabilities spectrum: ADD, ADHD, & LD.* (pp. 241-254). Baltimore: YorkPress.

Bender, M., Valletutti, P., & Baglin, C. A. (1998). *A functional curriculum for teaching students with disabilities: Interpersonal, competitive job-finding and leisure time skills* (Vol. four). Austin, TX: Pro-Ed.

Compton, D. M., & Iso-Ahola, S. (Eds.) (1994). *Leisure and mental health* (Vol. 1). Park City, UT: Family Development Resources.

Havens, M. D. (1992). *Bridges to accessibility.* Dubuque, IA: Kendall/Hunt.

Johnson, D. E., Bullock, C. C., & Ashton-Shaeffer, C. (1997). Families and leisure. *Teaching exceptional children,* pp. 30-34.

Mathews, P. (1977). Recreation and normalization of the mentally retarded. *Therapeutic Recreation Journal, 11,* 17-21.

Moon, M. S. (1994), The case for inclusive school and community recreation. In M. S. Moon (Ed.), *Making school and community recreation fun for everyone* (pp.1-13). Baltimore: Brookes

Wehman, P., & Schleien, S. (1980). Assessment and selection of leisure skills for severely handicapped individuals. *Education and Training of the Mentally Retarded, 15,* 50-57.

CHAPTER 4
Recreational Opportunities for Families of Young Children with Disabilities

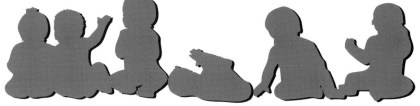

Dr. Brenda Hussey-Gardner, Terry Morrill Woodward, CTRS, Marjorie Shulbank, Mona Freedman

All families, whether or not they have a child with a disability, enjoy spending leisure time together. Although it may be a bit more challenging to discover activities in which the whole family can participate, recreation and leisure are an important aspect of a healthy lifestyle.

All individuals have a right to leisure to enhance the quality of life. Everyone is entitled to a broad spectrum of leisure services in the most inclusive setting. The term "inclusion" means that individuals with disabilities are included with peers who do not have disabilities. In the inclusive setting, people of all abilities recreate together, with barriers both physical and attitudinal removed. Inclusive leisure opportunities celebrate diversity, and encourage the community to accept and understand differences in individuals. Recreational opportunities are increasingly accessible for individuals with disabilities providing greater opportunities for families to recreate together, while including their child with a disability.

Where to Find Recreational Opportunities for the Whole Family

Department of Recreation and Parks

This is a good place to start on your search for recreational opportunities. Some of the programs one can expect to find are general recreation programs, arts and crafts, gymnastics, trips and tours, outdoor recreation, special events, the arts, cooking, family activities, and sports, among others. There are various programs for every age group. Several Recreation and Parks' Councils publish a Guide to Fun and Fitness which is distributed three times a year. This guide has an extensive listing of classes and programs with a description, date, time, place, and age group. Also found in this guide is a listing of Therapeutic Recreation programs, if you choose to have your child in a group with other children who have disabilities. These programs are conducted by certified professionals who have training in working with individuals with disabilities. It is helpful to have this choice for certain programs, and the choice for inclusive settings as well. The National Recreation and Parks Association (NRPA) is a resource on the internet and in the library to access specific issues related to parks and recreation. There are 11 branches and sections, and five regional offices for specific concerns. The National Therapeutic Recreation Society (NTRS) is one of these sections, and may be helpful in answering questions about programs for children with disabilities. Inclusion practices are also explained if you need more information about this philosophy, and whether or not you choose it for your child.

YMCA

There are aquatic classes for infants and parents, and swimming instruction for all age groups and skill levels. This is a nice option in the winter months to keep a child's swimming skills current for the summer season and outdoor swimming activities. There are a variety of parent and infant and toddler programs to choose from that work on a number of skill areas and socialization opportunities. YMCA is a leader in the community-based health and fitness and aquatics' programs. The YMCA offers hundreds of programs including camping, childcare, family nights, and many more based on community need. There is a focus on strong families, and strong communities. Visit the YMCA of the USA at http//:www.ymca.net for more information, and specific programs in your local area.

Girl Scouts of USA

Girls join Girls Scouts of America as early as five years old. They can continue through the age of 17. Girl Scouts is the largest voluntary organization for girls in the world. The focus is on helping each girl be the best she can be in all areas of her life. Most troops are receptive to the idea of accepting children with disabilities; call your local troop and ask them about how they could include your child.

Boy Scouts of America

Your young son of six years can start with the tiger cubs in first through fifth grade, then on to Boy Scouts through age 18. The Cub Scouts is family centered, and you can enjoy full family participation. The focus is on becoming a good citizen.

Library

Your local public library has programs that can be enjoyed by the whole family. Many libraries publish a calendar of events that gives information on the activity, time, date, and age group served. There are storytelling groups for all ages; infants accompanied by a parent, pre-school and school age children. There are crafts groups, puppet shows, activities related to a story, music performances, clown shows, theme stories, and activities (for example: related to the weather, or about bugs). You may find programs that include dances and songs related to a certain culture, magic shows, and science demonstrations, and holiday theme activities. The list of programs available at your local library is endless, which makes it a very useful resource when planning for your child with a disability, and the entire family.

Sampling of general recreation options:
- Swim Clubs
- Playgrounds
- Parks
- Zoos
- Bowling Alley (with bumper guards in the gutter to help the toddler)
- Rollerskating Rinks
- Iceskating Rinks
- Ski Resorts
- Amusement Parks (kiddy rides)
- Theme Parks
- Discovery Zone, Playcenters
- Gymnastics such as Gymboree, Rebounders
- Horseback Riding
- Movie Theaters
- Children's Stage Theaters
- Circus
- State Fairs/Carnivals
- Beach Resorts
- Picnics
- Nature Walks
- Children's Concerts
- Children's Museums

The Internet

The World Wide Web is a treasure chest of information on recreational opportunities for the family. You need not have personal access to the internet on a home computer to take advantage of this invaluable resource. The public library has free access to the Web for the general public, and also has free demonstrations to learn quickly how to use the internet. For example, Infoseek:Kids will lead you to the Family.com site, and provide you with a wealth of activities by age and interest, such as arts and crafts, indoor, outdoor, for the two year old, five year old, etc.

You can even find summer day camps and programs in your area under the Local Affiliates section. *Home.disney.com* is another good resource for recreational ideas for your infant and toddler, and other children as well. There are a number of sites to explore on the internet to gain access to recreational and leisure ideas for the entire family, including your child who has a disability, to maximize positive experiences.

Specific programs for your child with a disability

There are so many wonderful programs devoted to your child who has special needs that pertain to their development and interests. Most times the whole family can take part in these programs.

Sampling of therapeutic program options

North America Riding for the Handicapped Association (NARHA). Therapeutic horseback riding provides a wide range of benefits. These include greater confidence and self-esteem, greater flexibility and better balance, and friendships made with the people who work with the individual, and of course with the horse itself. Another choice is Hippotherapy, which provides sensory input through the horses repetitive and rhythmic movements. Specially trained physical, occupational, and speech therapists utilize this medical treatment for individuals who have movement dysfunction, as well as cognitive, psychological, behav-

ioral and communication challenges. To find out more call (800) 369-RIDE.

Adapted Recreation and Sports Programs

Programs like these are within your local Department of Recreation and Parks, Therapeutic Recreation Services section. Some counties publish a Leisure Resources newsletter with program listings called 'Recreation opportunities for people with disabilities'. These types of programs are designed specifically for those with disabilities, family members, and friends. Examples of programs are: Adapted Bowling, starting as young as four with parents as participant helpers, score keepers, and siblings as fans. Adapted Snow Ski Lessons, Adapted Karate, Adapted Aquatics, etc. Also included are Creative Arts and Performing Arts Programs for individuals with and without disabilities. There are, in addition, classes only for individuals with disabilities. The key is choice. There are sign language classes for children and adults. There is a disability awareness program that educates the public of the needs and abilities of individuals with disabilities by visiting the schools and colleges. This program also offers individuals with and without disabilities activities to build self-esteem and self-confidence. This is an extremely useful resource and can be obtained by calling your local Department of Recreation And Parks.

The National Information Center for Children and Youth With Disabilities (NICHCY)

This national information referral center provides information on disability and disability-related issues for families, educators and professionals. For specific questions on related services, or an area of interest call (800) 695-0825 or e-mail *nichy@aed.org*. The website address is *http//:www.nichy.org/*. They offer publications on a wide variety of subjects related to disabilities, and many of these can be printed directly off the internet. They will also do information searches of their databases and library. NICHCY has listings of selected statewide organizations to refer you to organizations you are seeking in your particular area of the country.

Computer programs offer a vast array of learning and recreational opportunities for the very young. There are a number of software packages that can be used for every age group. The personal computer is a wonderful resource to utilize with your young child who has a disability. The skills that are learned are invaluable in every area of functional development. These include fine motor skills enhancement, reasoning and problem-solving skills, and educational and communication skills, among many others. Of course, good old fun is a major benefit for the child, and starts him or her on their way to learning to enjoy leisure from a very young age.

There is so much information and so many resources in our society today, the child who has a disability has every advantage and opportunity to take part in recreation and leisure opportunities with their families, and society at large.

Facilitating Recreation & Leisure Opportunities

Now that you have some idea of the recreational activities that are available and now that you know how to choose an activity that is right for you and your child, let's explore ways of facilitating each individual recreational experience to help make it a successful one. Recreation and leisure opportunities can be categorized as informal or formal, child or family. Informal recreational opportunities include such things as going to a playground, zoo, or museum. More formal recreation includes activities that are structured and led by a professional. Examples of more formal recreation include swimming lessons, summer camp, and guided tours. In addition to the level of formality, one can look at who is involved in the recreational activity. The activity may involve only the child with the disability or it may involve other members of the family. Child recreation includes those activities in which the child participates with individuals outside of the family. Family activities involve the child and at least one other

TABLE 4.1

Types of Recreation

TYPE OF RECREATION	Informal	Formal
Family	Zoo Indoor or outdoor playground Museum Beach or pool	Guided tour of park Parent-child play group Library story hour
Child	Any activities above occurring with the child and individuals outside of the family (e.g. friends)	Classes (e.g., art, swimming) Summer camp

member of the family. See Table 4.1 for specific examples of these various types of recreation.

Informal Recreational Activities

Informal recreational activities can be simple or complex, spontaneous or planned. Your child can engage in informal recreational activities with family members or with friends. Your neighbor may offer to take your child to the playground or you may plan an organized family vacation to an amusement park.

Informal Family

Informal family recreation may involve only you and your child or it may include other family members. Prior to taking your child and family on an outing to a new location, call ahead to find out important information. In addition to the basics of cost and hours, ask specific questions to ensure that the place is right for your child and his needs.

If your child is in a wheelchair, find out where the handicap accessible entrance is located. If your child is in a stroller, be sure to find out whether or not strollers are allowed inside the facility. If your child is very active and has a short attention span, determine if there is a play area that you can visit; if so, be sure to take frequent breaks to visit this spot while there.

When engaging in informal recreational activities with your child, remember to have fun! While you are having fun, remember to be responsive to your child. Observe his signals to determine if he is happy and wants to continue the activity or if he is unhappy and needs a change. Whenever possible, follow your child's lead. If you're at an indoor playland and your child wants to play in the balls, play in the balls. Show your child how to wiggle in the balls, how to throw a ball, how to match two blue balls. In addition to watching your child's signals, also watch your feelings. It's important that you have fun, too! If you are getting bored or frustrated alter your activity so that it is enjoyable for you as well. When other family members are also participat-

ing, you will need to read their signals too. Remember recreation and leisure should be fun for everyone. Everyone should have a turn doing what they want; this is particularly important if siblings are involved.

When playing with your child, make the most of opportunities using as many senses as possible: taste, touch, smell, hear, and see. At a petting zoo, let your child touch the animal, talking about how soft the fur feels; smell the animal, talking about how it is a little stinky; hear the sound the animal makes, and imitate it, and see the different colors on the animal. While enjoying an ice cream cone at the park, let your child taste the sweet ice cream, touch the cold with his finger, smell the flavor of the ice cream, hear the crunch of the cone, and see the ice cream drip as it melts.

Informal Child Recreation

Informal child recreation includes informal activities in which your child participates without another family member. Frequently, this includes a short outing with friends or extended family members. Since a family member will not be present, it will be important that you find out the plans of the others inviting your child to join them. You will probably be asking many questions. Once you are comfortable that your child will be safe and will have fun, make sure that the responsible adult understands any special needs of your child. This may include food allergies, carseat positioning strategies, and signals that your child uses to communicate. If you get the impression that this well-intentioned person is beginning to feel like she took on more than she can handle, you may have to offer to join them, at least for the first outing.

Formal Recreational Activities

Formal recreational activities involve a professional who serves as the leader of the activity. This person may be the swimming instructor, camp counselor, or the playgroup leader. Typically, these activities involve groups of people under the supervision of a professional. When registering your child to participate in a formal recreational activity, it is important that you also make arrangements to speak with the professional who will be in charge of the activity. When speaking with this individual, share your child's strengths and special needs. You should also use this time to discuss possible adaptations that may be necessary. During your conversation, determine whether or not additional contacts will be necessary and if so, make arrangements for talking to one another on a regular basis.

Formal Family

Formal family recreation includes formal activities in which your child participates with another family member. At a minimum, formal family recreation usually includes another family adult. This adult may be a parent, aunt, uncle, or grandparent. It may also be a teenage sibling or adult family friend. This type of recreation offers the advantage of having a person who is very familiar with your child present at all times.

Formal family recreation allows your child to have experiences with knowledgeable support. In addition to the family adult, one or more other family members may also participate.

On the first day of a formal family recreational activity, take the time to introduce yourself and your child to others in the group. When introducing your child, briefly mention his special needs and answer any questions that others may have. By introducing your child and his needs, you will remove the mystery and hopefully eliminate any anxiety.

During the activity, be responsive to your child. Observe him to determine his needs, interest, desire for change, or wish to continue. More obvious signs such as crying, screaming, smiling, and laughing will be easy to identify. However, it will be important that you also look for more subtle signs such as grimacing and gaze aversion that may show a need for change or gentle rocking and leaning forward which may tell you your child wants more. Watch for signs of frustration. When you notice that he is frustrated, give him more assistance so that he will experience success. In addition to watching his feelings, watch your feelings too. The recreational activities should be fun for you, too. If you're not having fun, make a change so that you also enjoy your special time together.

Formal Child

Formal child recreation includes formal activities in which your child participates without another family member. Frequently, this type of recreation involves some sort

---

TABLE 4.2

Helping Sally See During Playgroup

Sally and her father attend a weekly playgroup together. They really enjoy their special time together. To make playgroup as successful as possible for Sally, Dad spends 10 minutes after each playgroup talking with the leader about her plans for the next week. Together, they figure out which modifications are needed to accommodate Sally's visual limitations. Sally can see, but her distance vision is very limited. Sally can only see things that are within six inches of her eyes. Jane, the leader, tells Dad that next week she plans to teach the class a song about animals. She explains that the tape came with some wonderful pictures of the animals mentioned in the song. She notes that she is concerned that Sally won't be able to see the pictures as she holds them up for the group to see. Dad suggests that she or he photocopy the pictures so that he can hold a corresponding picture up close for Sally as Jane holds up the picture for the class.

of instruction. Examples include swimming lessons, music lessons, and art lessons. Your child may receive this instruction one-on-one or in a group setting. In addition to lessons, formal child recreation may also include activities such as child-only playgroups and scouting. Formal child recreational activities allow your child to experience independence and allow you some potentially free time.

Unlike formal family activities, there will not be another adult participating in the activity who knows the ins and outs of your child. Therefore, you may need to spend a little extra time with the instructor sharing your child's special needs and determining the instructor's level of comfort with the needs of your child.

Although your child cannot be refused admission to any activities because of his disability, the success of the experience may be correlated to the instructor's comfort level. If the instructor is uncomfortable, you may be able to find another instructor who is more comfortable. Sometimes, however, this is not possible or desirable. Under such circumstances, it will be important for you to offer helpful pointers. In addition, you can encourage the instructor to call your child's therapists for advice, or you can ask the therapist to write a brief note containing important information.

CHAPTER 5
Recreational or Leisure Activities and the Development of Cognition in Young Children with Disabilities

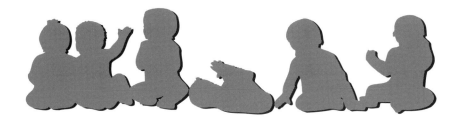

Janeen M. Taylor

The relationships parents have with their children are crucial to healthy child development in all realms. In the early years, children learn through their interactions with those who are nearest and dearest to them. When children feel safe and nurtured, learning is optimized. When children aren't sure what to expect from those in the environment, learning is inhibited.

Relationships Facilitate Learning

Did you ever go on a special outing with a parent or other relative? Perhaps you went to the beach with your family. Do you remember the weather? What size were the waves? Did you wade in the surf? What did you have for lunch? Did you fish? Did you catch any fish? Did anyone else? Chances are, you learned a lot on that special day and it is likely the emotional context of the day helped you retain many memories of

the events, setting, and people. A special outing has several of the features of a good learning experience. First, there are many interactions between adults and children. Second, everyone is focused on the same event and sharing a pleasurable experience. Lastly, there is plenty of time for children (i.e., those old enough to talk) to ask adults questions and adults have the time to respond fully and wait for further questions or reactions. These are some of the ingredients of a good learning experience (Greenspan, 1997). The trip was a fun, challenging, and interesting way to learn about relationships, the ocean, and other topics associated with a day at the beach. Let's explore the importance of relationships to cognitive development.

Social Relationships as a Foundation for Cognitive Development

Your child's first and most important social relationship is with you (Greenspan & Wider, 1997). The way you and your child interact has a profound impact on cognitive development. Manolson (1995) offers a number of simple suggestions for being a "tuned-in" parent and facilitating your child's learning. First, make sure you set aside a special time when you *allow your child to lead.* Observe your child and listen carefully to his or her attempts at communication. In doing so, you learn about such aspects of your child's personality as his or her likes, dislikes, concerns, and learning style.

Second, *be adaptable and share special moments* when they arise. When you stop an adult activity to interact with your child, you send the message that your child is important. By moving to your child's level (e.g., on the floor) and playing face to face, you let your child know that he or she is worthy of attention.

Third, *add new experiences and words* to your child's world. By carefully building on previous experiences, you can help your child develop a body of knowledge about a particular subject (e.g., zoo animals). By providing a new word for a person or object, you can cue a young child to the importance of language. You are your child's first and most important teacher and you can be more effective by following a few simple guidelines.

Turntaking in Relationships

An important aspect of social relationships is taking turns. Children must learn to take turns in conversations as well as during play. Learning how to take turns during interactions is important in both communication and relationships. It's hard for children to learn turn taking if they have few opportunities to practice. You can help your child learn how to take turns by setting up situations that call for turn taking. A game of "Peekaboo" is an early form of turn taking. Babies learn that when their parents' hands cover their faces, familiar sounds (i.e., "peekaboo") will occur next, and then it is the babies' turn for a special facial expression or sound that starts the game all over again. As your child matures, making brief statements that describe what you are doing, then allowing time for your child's re-

sponse helps your child understand the importance of turn taking, language, and communication. Your child's response may not be vocal, but may be a smile, eye contact, or an increase in motor activity to indicate an understanding of the notion of turn taking. Encourage these attempts at communication and build on any responses to conversations. These are important skills in cognitive development.

Your Child's Temperamental Style and Relationships

Each child is born with a unique personality, but there are general temperamental traits that many children share. Adapting a parenting style that complements your child's temperament will save you and your child much frustration (Bradway & Hill, 1993). For example, the child who is slow to warm up needs extra time to adjust to new situations, surroundings, or people. The child who reacts strongly to new situations and people often craves routine and predictability. Children who have intense responses to people, places, and objects may need transitional items for comfort during new events or situations. A beloved doll or blanket can be invaluable during family outings to new places. The best way to discover your child's temperamental style is to observe him or her during new situations, common activities (e.g., diaper changing), or with unfamiliar people. Notice when your child seems relaxed during these times and when your child appears to get upset by the person or event. Build on familiar experiences and relationships to slowly and carefully broaden your child's horizons (Brazelton, 1994).

Your Child's Relationships with Other Children

Children learn a lot about the world by socializing with other children. Understanding the various levels of play in which children engage is helpful in facilitating play with other children. Younger children tend to *play independently.* This is sometimes referred to as solitary play. They often engage in activities that do not seem to be related to those of other children in the area. Younger children may appear oblivious to the presence of other children, but if you watch closely, you'll probably notice that occasional glances or touches from one child to another signal the beginnings of more complex interactions that occur with more advanced levels of play. The next level of play still involves parallel activities, but the activities are more closely related. Both children may be playing with blocks, but each has a pile and is playing relatively independently. As children develop their cognitive abilities, they begin to increase their interactions with other children until they are ultimately engaging in true *cooperative play* (Linder, 1993; Rogers & Sawyers, 1993).

Cognition in Young Children

The development of cognition in young children is an incredibly complex phenomenon. Researchers, theorists, and practitioners cannot agree on one definition of cognition (Armstrong, 1993; Forman & Kuschner, 1983; Isenberg & Jalongo, 1997; Roopnarine & Johnson, 1993). Some child development experts believe that cognition involves primarily intellectual or mental abilities and processes. This view negates the effects of environment on cognition and emphasizes the nature side of the nature vs. nurture controversy (Vander Zanden, 1996). Others emphasize environmental influences on the development of cognition (Isenberg & Brown, 1997). Still others support the notion that both environment and heredity work in tandem to effect cognition (Safford & Safford, 1996).

Piaget and Cognition

Regardless of your definition of cognition and the development of cognitive skills, there are several concepts that appear to be central to cognition. Common to many of these concepts is the work of Jean Piaget. Piaget was a Swiss biologist who observed and wrote about children's construction of reality (Piaget, 1954). Piaget, emphasized the orderly, sequential nature of cognitive development in children (DeVries &

Kohlberg, 1987). Wolery and Wolery (1992) characterize Piaget's theories regarding intelligence as the "processes by which young children organize and construct their knowledge of the world" (p. 522).

In writing about cognition, Piaget (1969) used the term "schema" or "schemata" to refer to a person's understanding of a concept. One of Piaget's basic principles was that simple schemas are acquired prior to development of more complex schemas. Another critical Piagetian concept is the importance of children's active participation in the intellectual growth process. He often underscored the importance of active, rather than passive, involvement in learning. Allen and Marotz (1994) built upon Piaget's theories to suggest that cognition in young children involves "discovering, interpreting, sorting, classifying, and remembering" (p. 19).

Behaviorism and Cognition

Neisworth and Buggey (1993) stressed that "most behavior is learned" (p.115) and emphasized the importance of environmental support, also known as behaviorism, for mastery of knowledge and skills. They described the two fundamental principles of behaviorism as (a) "behavior is controlled by its consequences" and (b) learning depends on its outcome" (p. 118). Such concepts as rewards, punishment, and practice are critical features of behavioral theory and apply to many types of skill acquisition (e.g., learning to dance, learning to ride a bicycle).

Contemporary researchers are beginning to examine brain growth and development as they relate to cognitive development (Thatcher, Lyon, Runsey, & Krasnegor, 1996; Van Pelt, Corna, Uylings, & Lopes del Silva, 1994). Shore (1997) provides an extensive overview of this topic and offers a number of suggestions. Shore emphasizes that neurological (i. e., the brain) growth is positively affected by *healthy environments and experiences* in the early years. During the first four years of a child's life, important neurological connections are being developed. These connections are of

TABLE 5.1
Selected Principles of Cognitive Development

- Acquisition of basic skills or concepts usually occurs before more complex skills or concepts are acquired
- Schema building or scaffolding on familiar ideas is crucial to understanding more complex concepts
- A child's active participation is important to the learning process
- Motivation or rewards can facilitate learning
- Remembering is an important skill in cognition
- Practicing any skill will improve the chances of retention

better quality and more numerous when a child has consistent interactions with people and surroundings.

Another important issue in neurological development is *repetition.* Practice of desired behaviors supports development of strong neurological pathways. Whether the activity is walking, talking, or looking at books, children need innumerable repetitions to master a skill.

Neuroscientists have also established that there are critical periods when the brain is more or less vulnerable to environmental influences. Prior to birth and in the early years of life, the brain is especially vulnerable to injury or neglect. Providing rich experiences and a safe environment is essential to optimal brain development (Sylwester, 1995).

Stress and excitement can have a negative impact on brain development. Having an environment that is too stimulating or too noisy can keep a child in a hyperalert or stressed state. Be sure to have *quiet times and quiet areas* of your home so your child can spend some time in a low-stress environment. This allows a child to rest and recover from exciting or highly stimulating experiences (e.g., a trip to a crowded shopping mall). By the way, this is important for parents as well as children. You may want to make sure there is a least one area of your home designated as the quiet spot where children or adults can re-

gain balance and perspective after busy periods of the day or evening (Sargent, 1999). Additional suggestions provided by Shore (1997) are offered in Table 5.2.

Families of young children with disabilities and recreation

Because children with disabilities have special treatment needs, greater amounts of family time may be devoted to doctor's appointments, special instruction, speech therapy, occupational therapy, physical therapy, health care, and general caretaking activities. With demanding schedules, less time is available to families of children with disabilities for recreation and entertainment than to families whose children are not disabled (Bounds, Huett, & Powell, 1999).

Sarah's Family

Sarah is three years old and has cerebral palsy. She has one older brother who is six years old and a younger sister who is an infant. Sarah needs to be placed in specific positions for play, meals, story book reading, and other daily activities. Sarah wears braces, so her parents spend time every morning and evening helping Sarah into her braces. Sarah's eating, bathing, dressing, and toileting are especially time consuming for Sarah and her family. Since Sarah uses leg braces and a walker, she cannot get around very quickly, so her family

---

TABLE 5.2

Suggestions for promoting cognitive development

- Make sure your child has regular health care checks
- Make sure your home is a safe environment for your child to explore rooms, objects, and people
- Validate your child's feelings and attempts to communicate by responding to verbal and nonverbal cues
- Back off when a child seems to have enough stimulation or interaction
- Support your child by remembering that a child's temperament and style are unique
- Talk, read, and sing to your children to provide a language rich environment and a platform for communicative competence and literacy
- Encourage healthy relationships with other children to build a solid foundation of social skills
- Use mistakes as teachable moments
- Establish routines to reinforce everyday concepts and activities

---

uses a special stroller for Sarah and her baby sister when they are on an outing. There is little discretionary family time after routine child rearing chores, therapy appointments, health care provider visits, and other related activities. What time is available for family outings must be carefully planned to ensure that destinations are accessible to individuals with disabilities. Trips for Sarah's family require planning and patience. Family recreational outings are not impossible, but they do require effort and organization.

Using Family Recreation to Facilitate Cognitive Development

There are lots of ways for families to participate in recreational activities. Some are easier than others. Some require extensive planning and perseverance. Most recreational activities are enjoyable and provide many happy memories for a family (Marzollo, 1977). Here are a few suggestions for making the most of special family events.

Plan Ahead

Just as having the right tool can be critical to the successful completion of a home improvement project, having the right child-related items can be crucial to your child's enjoyment of a family outing. You might want to check the weather report well before leaving the house. Consider taking layers of clothing (i.e., to allow for weather changes), extra snacks (e. g., for unexpected delays in traffic), a change of clothes in case of toileting or other accidents, pacifiers or other important comfort items, and extra diapers. Be sure to figure out how you'll accommodate any security items your child finds important. A special blanket or doll can help alleviate any fear of going to a new place or trying a new activity (Galinsky & David, 1988). Additional suggestions for planning an outing can be found in Table 5.3.

ABCs of Family Fun Times

The following are 26 suggestions for family recreational activities. By using the suggestions described previously, all of these suggestions are designed to support your child's cognitive development.

A: *A stitch in time saves nine.* How many times have you heard this old adage? It is especially meaningful when you have a child with a disability. Any family outing can take a great deal of planning, but an outing that has been well planned can be especially fun.

B: *Become a scientist.* Observe your child and note responses to people, activities, places, and times of day. Whatever delights your child is reinforcing and whatever causes tears and tantrums is not fun for your child. It doesn't mean you have to abandon a new activity because you are unsure of your child's possible response, but take it slow and help your child adjust to new people, activities, and places. Some children are easygoing and don't mind new faces, places, or objects. Others take a while to warm up to new experiences.

C: *Catch and toss.* Playing with a soft (i.e., foam rubber) ball can be a great indoor or outdoor game. There are a number of adaptive balls and mitts containing velcro to assist beginning athletes with catching skills. Talk about who has the ball, who is throwing the ball, who is catching the ball, and "oops . . . we dropped the ball" to reinforce that words can describe actions, objects, and people. Large motor skills also help with the development of connections in the brain used for thinking skills.

D: *Drive to an ice cream stand.* Take a short drive to an ice cream stand. Show your child a photograph of an ice cream cone or dish of ice cream to introduce the activity. Let your child hold the picture on the way to the store and talk about where you are going. If you have an instant camera, take a picture of your child with his or her cone or dish of ice cream. Use the photograph at home to help your child recall the trip. Be sure to plan similar trips to reinforce such concepts as "going", "car" (i.e., or bus), "ice cream", "eating", "all gone", "going home".

E: *Even Mommies (i.e., or Daddies) sometimes make mistakes.* Just as Viorst (1973) indicated in her classic children's book about zombies, ghosts, and other scary things, "sometimes even mamas make mistakes". When you make a mistake in front of your child, be sure to admit it and point out the silliness (i.e., assuming there are silly aspects of your error) of your mistake. This helps your child understand that everyone makes mistakes. Mistakes can be wonder-

---

TABLE 5.3

Checklist for fun and cognition

- Do I have an approved car seat for my child; is it properly installed?
- Have I packed the right equipment (e.g., stroller)?
- Have I packed a change of clothes, warm clothes, and an umbrella?
- Have I packed extra diapers and wipes?
- Have I packed snacks/drinks?
- Have I packed security items (e.g., favorite blanket, and pacifiers)?
- Have I packed books that emphasize the key concepts of the activity (e.g., animal books for a trip to the zoo)?
- Have I packed tapes of songs that that emphasize key concepts of the activity (e.g., songs about animals)?
- Have I packed film and/or blank videotapes?
- Have I packed plastic bags for soiled items and trash?
- Have I prepared an alternate plan in case there is a problem?

ful opportunities for learning and for a good laugh. But be sure that your laughter is mutual, not hostile (e.g., not making fun of anyone for an error). Mistakes are wonderful learning opportunities for children and adults.

F: *Flexibility is important.* Regardless of the level of planning for any event, there is always the possibility of an unforeseen event. The event may be minor or more significant, but parental flexibility is a critical factor to the success of any family excursion.

G: *Go easy during transitions.* Transition times are very difficult for some children. Developing a routine for transitional times can smooth the way. A variation on a favorite song can be useful. For example, "this is the way we get in the car, get in the car, get in the car — this is the way we get in the car — so early in the morning", sung to the tune of "This is the Way We Wash Our Hands" can help familiarize your child with the routines associated with transitional times (e.g., going to and from the grocery store).

H: *Have a beginning, middle, and end.* There are three important phases to a terrific recreational experience. First, set the stage for a special time. Talk to your child about what you are going to do and see. Second, during the event, talk about what you are doing and seeing. Relate your activities to familiar or similar activities. This is called "schema building" and uses what your child already knows to develop a new level of understanding about a particular idea or event. Third, after you get home, talk about what you did and saw. Reinforce the most important parts of your recreational activity during your chats.

I: *If at first you don't succeed, try again.* When a family outing to a particular place (e.g., a local farm) is a flop, don't worry, you'll probably be able to try the same outing at a later date when your child is older, has developed more acceptable behaviors, or has a better understanding of the significance of the event. Try not to blame yourself or your child and remember there will be other special times.

J: *Just in case of an unexpected situation, have a back up plan.* If you've ever seen one of Chevy Chase's movies about his family's attempts at vacations, you know that the unexpected can happen. The zoo may be unexpectedly closed for landscaping, the Aquarium may be closed for repairs to the shark tank, or the park sprinklers may have malfunctioned and stayed on all night, leaving the playground a muddy mess. It's always a good idea to have an alternate plan in mind. A quick change of direction from the park to the airport observation deck or local children's petting zoo can save the day. Keeping a packet of brochures for local attractions in the glove compartment of your car can be very helpful when choosing a new destination for a family outing.

K: *Keep activities short and simple.* In keeping with your child's developmental age, temperament, and stamina, plan trips that are short and focus on a major event. For example, a trip to the zoo can have big cats or monkeys as the central theme. Should weather or child-related issues (e. g., fussiness, a fever) lead to a shortened excursion, at least the most important animals have been seen and discussed.

L: *Living room picnics can be magical.* You don't have to go far to have a family outing. Turn your living room into a park (i.e., this is especially appropriate on a rainy day), lay out a blanket, use paper plates, use plastic cups, and have a picnic. Talk about what you are doing. Point out little events associated with picnics. "First we open the picnic basket", "look at the round plates", or "feel the soft napkins" are ways of helping a child understand the various activities of a picnic.

M: *Make hay while the sun shines.* Take advantage of serendipitous good weather or lulls in your busy family schedule. A quick trip to a local park or museum can be fun and educational. With local maps and brochures of interesting locations in the glove compartment, you can pick a spot for a quick family outing.

N: *No place like home.* Having special times and routines at home can be as important to young children as an outing. Baking cookies, singing familiar nursery rhymes, reading books that are designed for your child's developmental level, or having a pretend tea party can all help your child develop cognitive skills and nurture your relationship with your child.

O: *One activity at a time.* One way to guarantee tears or tantrums is to try and pack too many events or trips into one outing. Unless you have an unusually quiet and relaxed child, multiple activities or trips will take a toll on your child's ability to maintain his or her composure.

P: *Pictures are worth lots of words.* Photographs of you and your child taken during special times allow your child the pleasure of reliving events. Looking at photographs reinforces memories of people and places. Label each photograph with people's names or a simple word (e. g., "play ground"), place in a simple album, and use the album as a book. Don't be surprised if your child begins to name the event, person, or place as you point to each picture. Looking at photograph albums provides a sound foundation for later reading activities.

Q: *Quit while you are ahead.* Even if you or your child are having a good time, if either of you tires or becomes irritable, you might want to end your excursion a bit early and head for home. Memories of a family experiences will be far more pleasant if they are short and sweet, whereas a trip involving whining or crying (by either you or your child) can become a disagreeable recollection.

R: *Repetition helps retention.* Repeat visits to a special place help your child develop an understanding (i.e., schema) for a particular subject. For example, don't stop at one trip to the farm. Plan many visits to farms and reinforce previously learned concepts. To further help your child retain memories of a wonderful experience, relate activities in the home to recreational experiences. For example, bake tree-shaped cookies before or after a hike or play with toy trains after a trip to a railroad museum or station.

S: *Safety first.* Don't let an event be ruined by an accident that could have been prevented. Use seat belts, use safety harnesses, use safe equipment (e.g., strollers), and keep alert for any potentially dangerous situations (e. g., unleashed dogs).

T: *Talk about what you are going to do; talk about what you are doing; talk about what you did.* Talk, talk, talk to your child. Use short and simple sentences to describe what will occur, describe what is happening, and describe what just happened. This helps your child sort out the myriad of experiences each day. Be sure to pause between statements to allow your child to process the information and be sure to acknowledge your child's attempts at communicating with you.

U: *Umbrellas can be lifesavers.* Don't forget to pack the umbrella. You might want to keep one in your car, one in the house, and a small travel umbrella in the diaper bag. Having an umbrella along can keep an outing from being a complete washout.

V: *Vary the pace.* Vary the pace of an outing. Allow down times between exciting experiences. If you are at a county fair and walking around the midway with its many sights, sounds, and smells, take periodic breaks and sit on a bench in a quiet area to regroup and discuss the day thus far.

W: *Wear washable clothes.* It is hard to spend time with young children and not have your clothes smudged or splashed. Wearing washable, casual clothes will take the worry out of the inevitable spills and messes that are common around children.

X: *X marks the spot.* As soon as your child is old enough, teach him or her your home phone number. This can be a nightly game of singing your phone number or making up a silly poem to rhyme containing your phone number. This bit of preparation will save a lot of worry should you and your child become separated in a crowd.

Y: *Yards can be jungles.* Don't forget that the back yard can be a wonderful place of adventure. Although not all families have back yards, if you are lucky enough to have one, be sure to make it as safe as possible and then figure out ways of making the yard a wondrous place for children. Children's play equipment can be purchased new, bought at a yard sale, or made by a handy parent. Be sure you check every angle for safety. The National Association for the Education of Young Children has marvelous resources regarding play equipment (see the Appendix B for the address of this organization). Help your child learn to use each part of the yard. A sand box is a great place to spend time with your child. A tire swing can provide hours of fun and important practice in balancing. There are also a number of companies that offer adapted play equipment. See the Appendix for suggestions of makers of play equipment. Be sure to make areas that are suitable for more than one child so that your child can have a friend over for an afternoon of play

Z: *Zoos are worth many visits.* There are so many educational opportunities at a zoo that you and your child could visit a zoo many times and see something new each visit.

Parental Well Being

With a positive parent-child relationship in combination with activities that support the cognitive development of children, much can be accomplished. Another issue that is important to address is your health and well being. A variety of researchers and practitioners believe that parental health and well being are key factors in child health and development (Beckman, 1996; Gallagher & Vietze, 1986; Greenspan, 1997; Fewell & Vadasy, 1986). Before starting regular family outings or other recreational activities, check your physical and mental health. Although adequate rest, proper nutrition, sufficient exercise, and time for spiritual renewal may seem like unattainable goals for parents of young children, it is worthwhile to examine these aspects of daily life and try to incorporate them into daily routines. Going on a trip to the zoo may not be the best use of a family's day

when a mother, father, foster parent, or other primary caretaker is so tired that he or she risks falling asleep at the wheel of the drive to the zoo. Taking care of yourself is important to you, is important to your child, and is important to your adult relationships.

Tending your own health

There are numerous books, magazine articles, and other written, audio, or video material with suggestions for increasing your health and well being. If you are interested in reading about ways to support your own health, check out the books and tapes in the health, family, or self-help sections of a bookstore, library, on-line bookstores (i.e., accessible through the internet), or some of the internet web sites listed in the Appendix of this book.

Hints for health

In his delightful book about health, Magaziner (1999) offers a number of ideas for healthy living. Try one of these suggestions, and if it works, try another. If it's not right for you, look elsewhere for guidance, but remember how important your health is to you and your relationship with your child or children. Magaziner suggests limiting your intake of refined or processed foods (e. g., sugar). Many are devoid of nutrition. Eat a variety of fresh fruits and vegetables to ensure consumption of a range of vitamins and minerals. Take time to relax or meditate every day, even if it is only for a few minutes. You recharge your batteries when you take a quiet break and may very well support your immune system's ability to fight illness. Get a good night's sleep. It's hard to be a good problem solver when you are sleep deprived.

Summary

Long after recreational activities are over, your relationship with your child will be central to your child's growth and development. Remember to have fun together and build memories to savor in the future. Having a loving, positive relationship can be the main ingredient in of a lifelong love of learning. And when an event is no longer fun, build in an "escape hatch". How will you get home if our child falls apart (e.g., has an unusually difficult tantrum), the crowds are much larger than anticipated, the noises and sights are overwhelming, or another unforeseen event mars a well-planned family event? Do you know the shortest route back to your house? Do you know an alternate route home in case your customary route is blocked by a parade or traffic accident? Considering these issues ahead of time can save you and your family the misery of trying to console an inconsolable child.

References

Allen, K., & Marotz, L. (1994). *Developmental profiles: Pre-birth through eight* (2nd ed.). Albany, NY: Delmar Publishers.

Armstrong, T. (1993). *Seven kinds of smart: Identifying and developing your many intelligences.* New York: A Plume Book.

Beckman, P. J. (Ed.). (1996). *Strategies for working with families of young children with disabilities.* Baltimore, MD: Paul H. Brookes.

Bounds, B., Huett, H., & Powell, H. (1999). *Who are the people in your neighborhood: Resource and referral support for the RECCs.* Session presented at the annual meeting of the Maryland Infants and Toddlers Program, Baltimore, MD.

Bradway, L., & Hill, B. A. (1993). *How to maximize your child's learning ability: A complete guide to choosing and using the best games, toys, activities, learning aids, and tactics for your child.* Garden City, NY: Avery Publishing Group.

Brazelton, T. B. (1994). *Infants and mothers: Differences in development* (rev. ed.). New York: Delacorte Press.

DeVries, R., & Kohlberg, L. (1987). *Constructivist early education: Overview and comparison with other programs.* Washington, D.C.: National Association for the Education of Young Children.

Fewell, R., & Vadasy, P. (Eds.). (1986). *Needs and supports across the life span.* Austin, TX: Pro-Ed.

Forman, G. E., & Kuschner, D. S. (1983). *The child's construction of knowledge: Piaget for teaching children.* Washington, D.C.: National Association for the Education of Young Children.

Galinsky, E., & David, J. (1988). *The preschool years: Family strategies that work — from experts and parents.* New York: Ballantine Books.

Gallagher, J. J., & Vietze, P. M. (Eds.). (1986). *Families of handicapped persons: Research, programs, and policy issues.* Baltimore, MD: Paul H. Brookes.

Greenspan, S. I. (1997). The growth of the mind and the endangered origins of intelligence. Reading, MA: Addison Wesley.

Greenspan, S. I., & Wider, S. (1997). *Facilitating intellectual and emotional growth in children with special needs.* Reading, MA: Addison Wesley.

Isenberg, J. P., & Brown, D. L. (1997). Developmental issues affecting children. In J. P. Isenberg and M. R. Jalong (Eds.), *Major trends and issues in early childhood education* (pp. 29-42). New York: Teachers College Press.

Isenberg, J. P., & Jalongo, M. R. (1997). *Major trends and issues in early childhood education.* New York: Teachers College Press.

Linder, T. W. (1993). *Transdisciplinary play-based intervention: Guidelines for developing a meaningful curriculum for young children.* Baltimore, MD: Paul H. Brookes.

Magaziner, A. (1999). *The complete idiot's guide to living longer and healthier.* New York: Alpha Books.

Manolson, A. (1995). *You make the difference: In helping your child learn.* Toronto, Ontario: A Hanen Centre Publication.

Marzollo, J. (1997). *Supertot: Creative activities for children one to three and sympathetic advice for their parents.* New York: Harper Colophon Books.

Neisworth, J. T., & Buggey, T. (1993). Behavior analysis and principles in early childhood education. In J. L. Roopnarine & J. E. Johnson (Eds.), *Approaches to early childhood education* (2nd ed.). New York: Merrill.

Piaget, J. (1954). *The construction of reality in the child.* New York: Ballantine Books.

Piaget, J. (1969). *The language and thought of the child.* New York: World.

Rogers, C. S., & Sawyers, J. K. (1993). *Play in the lives of children.* Washington, D.C.: National Association for the Education of Young Children.

Roopnarine, J. L., & Johnson, J. E. (Eds.). (1993). *Approaches to early childhood education* (2nd ed.). New York: Merrill.

Safford, P. L., & Safford, E. J. (1996). *A history of childhood and disability.* New York: Teachers College Press.

Sargent, M. C. (1999, December). *The impact of brain research on play-based intervention.* Paper presented at the meeting of the 15th Annual Division of Early Childhood International Conference on Children with Special Needs, Washington, D.C.

Shore, R. (1997). *Rethinking the brain: New insights into early development.* New York: Families and Work Institute.

Sylwester, R. (1995). *A celebration of neurons: A classroom teacher's guide.* Alexandria, VA: National Association of Secondary School Principals.

Thatcher, R. W., Lyon, G. R., Runsey, J., & Krasnegor, N. (Eds.). (1996). *Developmental neuroimaging: Mapping the development of the brain and behavior.* San Diego, CA: Academic Press.

Van Pelt, J., Corna, M. A., Uylings, H. B. M., & Lopes del Silva, P. H. (Eds.). (1994). *The self organizing brain: From growth cones to functional networks.* New York: Elsevier Science Ltd.

Vander Zanden, J. W. (1996). *Human development* (6th ed.). New York: McGraw-Hill.

Viorst, J. (1973). *My mama says there aren't any zombies, ghosts, vampires, creatures, demons, monsters, fiends, goblins, or things: But sometimes even mamas make mistakes.* Hartford, CN: Altheneum.

Wolery, M., & Wolery, R. A. (1992). In D. B. Bailey, & M. Wolery (Eds.), *Teaching infants and preschoolers with disabilities* (2nd ed.) (pp. 521 - 572). New York: Merrill.

CHAPTER 6
Adaptive Approaches to Recreation and Leisure Activities for Infants and Toddlers

Ginny Popiolek

Play is a voluntary act that is initiated during free time and can be stopped and started at any time. It is the active use of leisure time, which has a beginning and an end. A toddler decides to "cook" dinner for his mom. The pretend meal is made with great care and detail and given with pride to mom. This play interaction is completed by the child's choice. These qualities of play present many opportunities for developmental intervention infants and toddlers with disabilities.

Children play for many reasons—intrinsic motivation, curiosity, imitation, fun, control, and most of all, to learn. This learning environment for children cannot be neglected or overrated for its value. Through play the toddler/learner is encouraged to experiment in a risk-free environment. Play is interactive and provides cause and effect experiences for learning the tasks of daily life. Appendix C provides a variety of leisure activities. These experiences offer children the opportunity to make choices and begin

to control their world, e.g., "Should I stand up and play with the toy on the couch or sit on the floor and play with the blocks?" Children who don't play and experience the feelings of control in their lives may feel helpless without a decline in self-esteem (Rogers & Sawyer, 1988).

Play permits the child to select the level of difficulty and the intensity of the activity. This promotes success with learning and thus the desire to continue or repeat the activity at another time, which is an example of intrinsic motivation. When children are intrinsically motivated, praise and rewards are not necessary to continued play. The joy and reinforcement of the play provide the motivation.

According to Piaget (1962), from birth to approximately two years of age, children are in the sensory-motor development stage of learning. During this stage, learning occurs through: touching, hearing, feeling, seeing, and tasting, in combination with a motor activity. Babies reach for things they see, turn their heads to sound, grab and bite foods that they smell, and move their hands away from objects that are offensive to touch. The play style they use during this stage is practice play—repetition of behavior until it is learned. Practice play can be cognitive as well as motoric and permits errors in a positive manner. If the child does not reach the object there is no negative consequence, instead the child will usually attempt to continue to move and reach to accomplish the goal.

The preoperational stage of learning, approximately ages two through seven, presents a play style called symbolic play. Symbolic play requires children to understand time and sequence, role playing, and the roles of other individuals. Children demonstrate this stage through routines in daily living, imitating behaviors (cook, fireman, and in playing house).

Finally, concrete operational development occurs between ages one and twelve and manifests itself in play with rules of a game. Winning and losing a game does not appear to be of concern until approximately seven or eight; previous to this age children play for the joy of playing. These three stages of play culminate to develop more complex play.

How can we help our children play?

The value of play as use of leisure time in the development of children with disabilities, appears clear. The challenge is "how can we as educators, parents, and friends assist in its promotion?" The nature of disabilities are various and create diverse challenges. Topical components related to the use of leisure will be addressed with materials and suggestions. In this manner, individual issues can be selected by the reader.

The Child

The most important component in addressing the leisure needs of children with disabilities is knowing the child—his needs and preferences. Leisure time, by definition, is a period of time in which activities of the individual's preference are engaged in for a duration of her choice.

Systematic observation of the child's behavior is the first step. Children with disabilities, especially with severe delays, do not often spontaneously play or show enjoyment. Normal development of an infant one to four months old, includes smiling and laughing spontaneously in response to pleasurable sights and sounds.

Reaching for objects may occur at about three to four months and simple social behaviors at five to ten months. Children with severe disabilities frequently demonstrate diminished expressions of pleasure and social skills, if they are present at all. They often engage in fewer activities and spend a great deal of time lying on their back or sitting (Burstein, 1986). For this reason, a structured observation of the child should be completed.

Below is an assessment profile that will assist in identifying preferred components for leisure activities. The use of this checklist is to identify appropriate leisure activities and environments that are most conducive to enjoyment for the individual child.

Child Profile for Leisure Activities

Materials for Leisure Activities

Free time or playtime is a period of time for children to choose a "fun" activity—to take a break. The choices children make to utilize their leisure time change quickly with their age. As children grow older, their play becomes more skilled and sophisticated. These premises are also true for children with disabilities.

Toys in our stores are initially grouped by children's chronological age—infant, toddler, preschooler and then later by interests—trucks, trains, dolls, games, etc. When selecting toys for a child with a disability, it is important to reflect on the child (see inventory)—interests, motor ability, dislikes, as well as cognitive and developmental stages. The chart below should assist in correlating specific toys with stages of play.

TABLE 6.1
Checklist

Age: _____

Disability: _____

Easily separates from family members? ❑ Yes ❑ No

Interactions
❑ Eye contact ❑ Sits near ❑ Active ❑ Wants to be alone
❑ Engages peers/adults

Activity Preference
❑ Prefers ❑ Does not like
❑ Low Energy ❑ High Energy

Sensory Stimulation
❑ Lights ❑ Textures
❑ Noise ❑ Smell

Time with Activity
❑ Stays with activity more than 5 mins.
❑ Switches activity frequently
❑ Engages in activity with adults/children
❑ Needs assistance to engage in an activity

Motor Ability
❑ Can be positioned ❑ Needs assistance
❑ Enjoys independence
❑ Prone ❑ Supine ❑ Side lie ❑ Sits
❑ Rolls ❑ Crawls ❑ Kneels ❑ Stands
❑ Walks ❑ Runs

Communication
❑ Attempts ❑ Uses ❑ Enjoys augmentative communication
❑ Low tech ❑ Devices eye contact ❑ Gestures
❑ Signs ❑ Babbles ❑ Words ❑ Short sentences

It is important to evaluate the appropriateness of a toy or activity. A four-year-old child with multiple disabilities who demonstrates limited motor ability could be playing with a switch-operated toy appropriate to his age rather than reaching for a mobile in front of him. The mobile is an excellent toy to stimulate reaching for an infant, but it is not appropriate to be utilized by a four-year-old child working on reaching. We must always question ourselves concerning the appropriateness of the toys and activities utilized with children. This issue becomes more overt as the child matures. For example, a 16-year-old student with multiple disabilities could work with a balloon for reaching and tracking but reaching and pushing a bowling ball using a ramp for independent bowling with a peer would be preferable and more age appropriate.

Questions we should ask ourselves concerning toys and other materials.

- **Is it safe?** Balloons when broken can be swallowed and therefore should be covered (Balzac—found in toy stores). Items may be too small for a small child or could carry a warning label.
- **Will this be overstimulating?** Children sensitive to sound, texture, etc. will need to have toys and activities carefully evaluated, yet a sensory diet needs to be provided.
- **Is this toy/activity at the child's level of functioning?** Use the correct seat for a swing in comparison to their motor ability.
- **Will this create the level of social skills appropriate to the child's ability?** Cooperative play, taking turns, parallel play, which situation is suitable to the child's affective level.
- **Does this need to be supervised?** Safety must always be the first priority.
- **Is this age-appropriate?** Is this activity or toy utilized with non-disabled peers. If the answer is no, why should this child be using the toy or activity?

Toys and environments promote different types of play and social demands on

TABLE 6.2

Stages and Toys

Sensory Experiences

colors	bright sheets	balls	high contrast sounds
rattles	chime ball	musical toys	reflection
mirrors	visual tracking	mobiles	textures
foam blocks	activity center	action/motion	pop-up toys
squeeze toys			

Movement and Active Play

riding	scooters	big wheels	rocking
swings	rocking horse	pushing/pulling	push carts
balls	carriage	tossing balloons	bean bags
sliding	sleds	slides/playground	sitting/activity
shape shorters	puzzles, beads	stacking	blocks
ring stacker	dramatic play	playing house	dolls
trucks	costumes	sensory	water play
sandbox	bean table	finger paint	rhythm
musical instruments	music box	tape player	movement to music

children. Below is a list of play types, behaviors, and toys that should assist in the programming of children with disabilities.

The Environment for Play and Leisure

Play and leisure activities for infants and toddlers with disabilities will occur in the home for the majority of the time. Opportunities may also be present in the community and school. In all these areas the environment is a critical component.

1. Is it motivating? Children with disabilities often do not demonstrate a curiosity or desire to interact with their environment. The surroundings in which an infant or toddler is placed for play and leisure can raise the child's level of alertness. This increase in their level of alertness encourages and prepares them for interaction. Therefore, materials should be:

- colorful and attractive—bright colors mixed with backgrounds of contrast will assist visually impaired children as well as motivate other children. An appropriate sensory diet that meets the child's individual sensory needs will help to maintain an optimal level of alertness for learning and playing.
- objects should be placed at the child's visual level—equipment and material for play should be placed for optimal visual stimulation. This concept may appear obvious, but the adult should place themselves on the floor in the same position as the child. This visual check will assure proper placement. Adults may be shocked at the perception of the world from the infant/toddler's point of view.
- objects and environment should be somewhat familiar—young children

TABLE 6.3

Programming

Type of Play	Behavior	Type of Toy
Solitary	• Reacts to people or stimuli • Demonstrates object permanence • Exploration of toy • Shows object preference	Jack in the box Hide and seek Activity box Choice making
Parallel	• Play space nearby • Aware of other children but no interaction • Imitates or leader-directed activity	Sand table Playground Sitting activity Simon says Toy phones Pretend toy lawnmowers
Associative/ Interactive	• Plays with others • Shares • Make believe • Takes turns	Playground, ball activities Board games Action figures Dolls
Cooperative	• Small group games • Uses simple rules	Parachute Hide and seek Tag

transition to new environments with objects and arrangements that are familiar. This assists in making the child feel secure. This is not to say that rooms should not be moved or that a toy selection should remain the same or new places not be visited. It is simply stating that all the above should not occur simultaneously. Allow the child some familiarity and explain to him what is happening. For example, "We are going to a new playground, but this playground has slides and swings just like the one we usually visit."

- environments should include choices—play and leisure activities should always include choices for children. Making choices develops self-esteem and confidence. These choices can be related to which activity or toy, alone or with a peer, and the duration of the activity. The environment facilitates all of these choices. It is important for us to observe the child's behavior. Often, it is her behavior that indicates the need for the environment to be altered to facilitate a choice; for example, pushing a child away to indicate he wants to be alone.

- the area that children play and/or recreate should always be SAFE—The activity and area should be carefully assessed and reviewed for safety. Medical information and contraindicated activity or positioning should be carefully reviewed with professionals. This information should be included in the choice-making of leisure activities. For example, latex intolerance has become an increasing concern for children with disabilities, and therefore materials and environment need to be carefully screened.

Play, Leisure and the Family

Siblings

Brothers and sisters have diverse and unique relationships. These relationships are the first social network a child is exposed to and frames the interactions with people outside the family. Each sibling within a family brings forth unique contributions to the family unit. This is especially true when a child with special needs is born.

The reaction of siblings to a sibling born with special needs is determined by various factors and combinations:

- age of sibling
- number of children in the family
- age difference of children
- financial status
- community support system
- type and severity of disability
- coping skills of family members
- interactions within family

The relationship of siblings to their brother or sister with a disability will be dynamic—playmates at first and friend, caretaker, protector, foe, or partner later. A positive relationship needs to be nurtured and developed through providing accurate information and meaningful interactions. Siblings need to know what is different about their brother or sister and why he or she is different. When families choose to not openly discuss this information, siblings allow their imagination to provide an explanation. This can only lead to complications. Play and leisure time activities provide a medium by which meaningful interactions can take place.

First, play interactions provide opportunities to demonstrate skills that an infant or toddler with a disability can perform as well as ones the sibling can help them complete. Secondly, it provides a time to interpret behaviors and communication and thereby increases the comfort level of their sibling. Anxiety related to the disabled sibling is also lowered by providing a comfortable environment to have fun. Thirdly, play and leisure provides a time where both children can receive feedback and attention from a parent or significant adult. Competition for attention is always a concern within a family unit. Validating each child's self-worth is critical and can be completed in a positive environment within a play situation. Finally, it provides a time where accurate information related to the disability can be clearly explained and often demonstrated through activity.

When a sibling is of school age, the play and leisure activity with the sibling with the disability is quite different. Pressure and teasing may be initiated at school. Brothers and sisters may not want siblings to be a part of the community activities—playground, pools, library, etc. Embarrassment may become a significant issue to address with the family. Parents, professionals, and others in the community need to respond by offering awareness programs within the school, answering questions, and providing information for children to assist in creating a more compassionate and knowledgeable environment.

Ideas for Sibling Recreation
- utilize parallel play
- adult-facilitated interactions using toys and/or games
- trips to community sites: playgrounds, zoo, story hours
- simple craft projects: start seeds-gardening, play dough, sponge paint, or finger paint (use pudding or whipped cream)

Parents and Extended Families

It has been stated repeatedly how important it is for the infant or toddler with a disability to be included in family activities. This is not an easy task but a critical one for both the family and the child. Normal family activity provides experiences in which infants and toddlers learn basic concepts related to language, social skills, and cognition. When children are excluded from these normal routines and experiences, a learning opportunity is missed. This is not to say that this is an easy task. Dressing, moving, feeding, and positioning is often a time-consuming and exhausting task and yet normalization of family activity assists in reducing resentment.

Below are some suggestions to assist with play and leisure activities:
- Allow child decision-making opportunities for play and leisure. This should be an activity that provides pleasure and fun.

- Toys and activities should be sensory rich. Allow children to touch, smell, and interact with animals, toys, flowers, children, etc.
- Materials and stimuli should be at eye-level and within visual field. You may need to lower objects or raise the child (take them out of the stroller) to ensure they are visually regarding the stimuli. It is helpful to place yourself at his level to give yourself the child's point of view—it is very different!
- When traveling contact the hotel and area visiting to communicate special needs. Many places will provide passes so you are not waiting in lines, as well as bathroom and feeding accommodations, adapted sleeping provisions, etc. for the family. You need to advocate for the needs of the child.
- Carry appropriate medical information and have a medical plan in place for where you are traveling. Communicate with the child's medical team so that there are no questions regarding protocol.

Comfort in managing children is critical to enjoying free time. Be aware of the appropriate time allotment for the child's attention. Structure participation in activities based on this information to assist in eliminating negative behaviors.

Suggested Community Activities
- Walks
- Visits to zoo, museum, library, and amusement parks
- Outdoor education area; estuary center, nature walks, hands on nature experience
- Toddler movement classes—be sure the instructor is aware of medical and instructional needs
- Playground
- Bicycling—various attachments and adaptations are available
- Aquatic experiences—lessons, riding in a boat/canoe with appropriate safety precautions

- Visits to farms—see animals and pick fruits and vegetables
- Therapeutic horseback riding

Contact the therapeutic recreation person through your local parks and recreation agency/organization for additional information.

Curricular Implications

Typical curriculum development for infants and toddlers with disabilities utilizes a "bottom-up" format that is completed with the assistance of developmental scales and assessments. This technique is effective for providing developmental information in the areas of language, gross and fine motor skills, cognition, social skills, as well as self-care. It is critical information to assist in the planning and programming, but it is not complete.

Curriculum development needs to expand to include an activity-based approach (Bricker, 1998) and top-down planning (Block, 1994). Activity-based learning as described in *An activity-based approach to early intervention* by Dr. Bricker, includes:

- Routine, planned or child-initiated activities
- Embedded goals
- Logical antecedents and consequences
- Generative, functional skills

Activity-based intervention targets skills that are functional, such as play and leisure skills, and develops these skills in a natural environment. Skill development is not taught in isolation. Objectives for all areas are embedded within the activities. Natural routines within the home or school are utilized to facilitate the learning.

A top-down approach assists in long-term planning when paired with an evaluation of functional skills. The team projects forward to elementary, middle, high school, and adulthood, to set long-term goals. These long-term goals are broken down into steps to assist in developing a vision and process for the child. This process is continually adjusted to meet the child's immediate needs; but it is critical to have a vision for where and what a child will be doing in the future. We do this unconsciously for our non-disabled children and yet forget to dream and plan for a child with a disability. This top-down approach encourages continually evaluation of the environment, adaptive skills, functional skills, community, and support system but most importantly, promotes long-term planning.

Curriculum for infants and toddlers with disabilities needs to expand to include a multifaceted approach. It is important to assess current levels of development to program in a functional, child-directed manner and to have a vision for the future.

Recreation and Leisure for Children with Disabilities

What I can do if I'm a parent:

- Include children with disabilities in all family activities whenever possible
- Have FUN with your family—laugh!
- Request the assistance and service of the adapted physical education teacher in the public school system.
- Contact the therapeutic recreation specialist in the parks and recreation department and ask about available programs.

What I can do if I'm a special education teacher:

- Provide practical information related to what the child is able to perform.
- Provide information concerning support groups and other services that can assist with understanding their child's disability.

What I can do if I'm in the medical profession:

- Provide information concerning contraindicated activities.
- Provide information related to equipment and techniques that may assist in normalizing family life.
- Provide emotional support.
- Make the time to answer questions

from individuals who are part of the support system or educational program.

What I can do if I'm an adapted physical education teacher or therapeutic recreation specialist:
- Provide information concerning programs for infants and toddlers with disabilities.
- Advocate for the development of appropriate programs and services.
- Assist in providing information concerning companies and places to purchase appropriate toys and equipment.
- Provide parent, family, and sibling workshops on play and leisure activities.

References

Attermier, S. M., Hacker, B. J., Jens, K. G., & Johnson-Martin, N. M., *The Carolina curriculum for infants and toddlers with special needs* (Second Ed.). Paul H. Brookes Publishing Company. Baltimore, Maryland, 1991.

Block, M. (1994). *Teacher's Guide to Including Students with Disabilities in General Physical Education*. Paul H. Brookes Publishing Company. Baltimore, Maryland, 1991.

Bricker, D. (1998). *An activity-based approach to early intervention.* (Second Ed.). Paul H. Brookes Publishing Company. Baltimore, Maryland.

Brown, Carla, & Brown, Kristie, (February 5, 1999.) "Visual Impairment and Early Motor Development". Teleconference presentation at Catonsville Community College.

Burstein, N. (1986). The effects of classroom organization on mainstreamed preschool children. *Exceptional Children, 52*(5), 425-434.

Clements, R. L., & Schiemer, S. (1993). *Let's move, let's play.* Kinder Care Learning Centers, Inc.

Cunningham, C., & Sloper, P. (1978). *Helping your exceptional baby.* Patheon Books, New York.

Grenot-Scheyer, M., Meyer, L. H., & Schuartz, I. S., (April, 1998). Blending best practices for young children: Inclusive early childhood programs. pp. 8-10. *TASH Newsletter.* Number 4.

Lake, D., Lilly, J., & Dinardo, J., (March, 1998). On vacation. page 26. *Exceptional Parent.* Vol. 28.

Mann, D. (Spring, 1996). Serious play. *Teachers College Record,* Vol. 97.

Meyer, D. J., (September, 1994). SIBSHOP: Workshop for siblings of children with special needs." pp. 47-49. *Exceptional Parent.* Vol. 24.

Murphey, K. H., (October, 1996). Toys the tools of play. pp. 31-34. *Exceptional Parent.* Vol. 26.

Piaget, J. (1962). *Play, dreams and imitation in childhood* (C. Gattegno and F.M. Hodgson, Trans). New York: Norton.

Rodgers, Crosby S., and Sawyer, Janet K. (Eds.). (1988). *Play in the lives of children.* Washington, D.C.: National Association for the Education of Young Children.

Schultz-Krohn, W. (July, 1997). Early intervention: Meeting the unique needs of parent-child intervention". pp. 47-59. *Infants and Young Children.* Vol. 10.

CHAPTER 7
Implementing Recreation and Leisure for the Young Child with Health in Mind

Renee Wachtel, MD

According to The American Heritage Dictionary (1), "recreation" is defined as "the refreshment of one's mind or body after work through some activity that amuses or stimulates". Yet for many families with a special needs child, the idea of refreshment for the child and/ or parent is frequently overlooked in the midst of competing time demands of therapy services, daily activities of the family, and various health care appointments. This is often to the detriment of the balance needed between work and play. The purpose of this chapter is to help families and providers consider the advantages of recreational activities for the infant and toddler with disabilities, and to highlight particular considerations that might relate to specific health conditions or disabilities.

Recreational activities can have many goals for the child, many of which are complementary to the child's early intervention program. For example, part of a child's social-emotional development involves learning socially appropriate interactive behaviors, including a variety of social skills that can be learned and practiced in recreational activities. It is the opportunity to practice newly learned developmental skills in natural environments that makes recreation an essential part of the child's social experience. Recreation therefore reinforces developmental skill acquisition, allowing the child to integrate skills learned in a therapeutic or different natural environment. Another important goal of recreation is to allow the child to explore the environment, with all the sounds, smells, and textures that the world may present. Since many recreational activities involve other children, perhaps with their siblings or parent, the child will have the opportunity to improve play skills, another developmental task. And finally, but probably most importantly, a major goal of recreation is to HAVE FUN!

Recreational opportunities are quite variable, ranging from informal play groups and family recreation to therapeutic recreational programs. While they may be targeted toward children with disabilities or be mainstreamed or inclusive, all families and providers should consider the medical status and special health concerns of the child during the planning stages of the activity.

For young children, there are many health issues that should be considered before embarking on a particular recreational activity. Some of these issues are applicable to all children in a variety of activities, and some are more specific to the particular health needs dictated by the child's medical status. Both sets of concerns should be thoroughly investigated prior to making final arrangements to avoid disappointments.

For infants and toddlers with chronic health problems that impact upon their ability to participate in recreational activities that typically developing children participate in, it is helpful for the early intervention team to establish an individual recreation plan. This plan should identify goals for the recreational participation, strategies to meet these goals, signs and symptoms to look for to detect health compromise early, and delineate appropriate responses if health compromise is detected. A variety of recreational activities should be identified for each child, including those requiring active and passive participation, if possible.

General Health and Safety Concerns

For all children with disabilities participating in recreational activities, the environment should not pose unnecessary risks to the health and safety of the child. For this reason, it would generally be appropriate to visit the site in advance, and review the safety checklist below:

1. Is the equipment well maintained, with no missing parts, excessive wear or rust?

2. Is safety equipment in place, and working (e.g. safety gates, electric outlet plugs)?
3. Are there sharp edges to the equipment, or unsafe materials used (e.g., non-safety glass)?
4. Are emergency exits and emergency equipment clearly marked and accessible?
5. Are hygienic practices used, (e.g., cleaning toys) between sessions?

It would also be wise to determine the staffing ratios and staff expertise, particularly if your child has special health care needs that might require specific handling, protection, or equipment. If licensing is required for a particular program, ask to see the license, to verify that it is current. Finally, it would be useful to determine their policy for participation of children with acute illnesses, and to get a sense of how consistently this policy is enforced.

Special Concerns About Infection

Many parents of infants and toddlers with disabilities, especially if their child has a special health care need, are very concerned about the potential of their child acquiring an infection during her participation in recreational activities. While this is clearly an appropriate concern, the risk must be weighed against the potential benefits to the child of participation. There are also many actions that the parent can take to minimize the risk of infection, both to the child and the parent.

Probably the most important action that all parents can take is to not bring their children to an activity if they are sick. Respecting the health needs of other children and families is an important issue, however inconvenient it may sometimes be. Encouraging handwashing, both between activities and after any contact with body fluids (e.g., diaper changes) is another important action. Finally, limiting the sharing of personal equipment, such as towels, will limit the spread of infection.

Special Concerns For Children With Specific Health Care Needs:

Congenital Heart Disease

Heart disease in children is relatively uncommon, occurring in approximately 0.8% of live births. However, certain conditions that cause developmental disorders also cause congenital heart disease. Genetic studies have shown that 5 percent of children with heart disease have a chromosomal abnormality, which may be associated with other physical defects and developmental delays. In addition, approximately 3 percent of children with congenital heart disease have a single mutant gene. In certain genetic disorders associated with developmental disabilities, up to 90% of children have congenital heart disease (such as Trisomy 13 or 18).

The most common type of heart disease associated with disabilities is a ventriculoseptal defect (an abnormal hole in the heart's inner wall that allows mixing of blood with and without oxygen), although multiple or complex congenital heart defects occur in a number of disorders as well. For some children, cyanotic heart disease is the result, where there is abnormal blood flow from or through the heart and decreased blood oxygen, causing an intermittent or constant bluish color to the normally pink lips and fingernails. This decreased blood oxygen can produce a significantly reduced capacity of the child to engage in physical activity, in addition to potentially causing cognitive or neurological impairment. For this reason, earlier surgical correction is frequently encouraged, if the heart abnormality is able to be corrected and the child is stable enough to endure the surgery.

Implications related to recreational activities fall into three categories. For one, determining whether the heart disorder compromises the child's endurance and ability to participate in physical exertion is essential. For some children, the heart disorder is severe enough to cause congestive heart failure, where the heart is unable to pump enough blood to keep up with the child's needs. This is generally treated with medications that reduce fluid overload and improve heart function, and with fluid restriction to limit the heart's burden. In many of these situations, additional physical exertion could cause further signs of heart failure, including shortness of breath or wheezing, sweating out of proportion to the environmental temperature, or swelling of the hands and feet. In extreme cases, if the heart failure is barely controlled with medication, even a prolonged crying episode can cause additional signs of heart failure. This does not occur, however, in most children with congenital heart disease whose disorder is well controlled with medication. For most children, reasonable amount of active participation is not only safe but encouraged. For this reason, it is essential for the team to consult with the child's physician to determine what degree of physical activity is permissible.

For children who have very limited physical activity permitted, passive participation in recreational activities is encouraged. For example, the child can be pushed in a swing, as long as the child is properly secured and supported in the seat. This enables the child to develop vestibular and postural responses to movement, as well as promoting social interactions.

If active participation is permitted, activity should be gradually increased over time, with careful monitoring for signs and symptoms of cardiac compromise (e.g., signs of heart failure, noted above). Therapists should clarify which parameters should be monitored, what acceptable levels of these parameters are, and what should be done if they are exceeded.

Another situation exists in children with congenital heart disease who are usually well, but have intermittent episodes of decompensation. These are children with complex heart disease such as the Tetralogy of Fallot (who have "Tet Spells," during which they suddenly turn blue and assume a squatting position), or have intermittent cardiac arrhythmia or irregularities in their heartbeat. For children in this category, it is important to determine in advance appropriate responses if any of these situations occur during the recreational activities, and whether there is any potential environmental trigger to be avoided.

Finally, many children with congenital heart disease are at risk for infectious complications of their heart disease, particularly bacterial endocarditis, an infection of the heart or the heart valves. Increasing tiredness, personality changes, irritability, or decreased endurance may be signs of this complication that should be immediately referred to the child's physician for further evaluation.

Pulmonary Disorders

Children with chronic pulmonary disorders may have intermittent symptoms, such as children with asthma, now commonly called reactive airway disease (RAD). They may show signs of rapid breathing, wheezing, or persistent cough during an exacerbation, which may be triggered by exercise, an upper airway infection, or allergies. In many cases, chronic treatment with nebulizers and/or oral medication prevents or minimizes symptoms. However, some children have infrequent problems and may only receive medication when signs of an asthma attack are noted.

For children with RAD, the recreation plan should identify any triggers for respiratory distress, especially if the child has allergies to dust, pollen, or grass. If exercise is a trigger, the child may need to take a nebulizer treatment before engaging in play activities that entail substantial physical exertion to minimize respiratory problems and to maximize potential benefit from the activity. Recreation locations should be selected to minimize exposure to potential asthmatic triggers. In any case, unless the child's physician prohibits active participation, the child should have graduated physical exertion with careful monitoring for respiratory problems. The goals of the recreational activity should include establishing methods of reaching maximal functional respiratory capacity over time.

Many infants and toddlers who were extremely premature at birth have chronic lung disease called bronchopulmonary dysplasia (BPD). In this condition, the child has required supplemental oxygen for a variable period of time, and may in fact still require oxygen for sleep, physical activities, or even 24 hours a day. In addition, many children with BPD are on nebulized medication, such as bronchodilators or steroids, or are treated with oral medication. The infants may also be on an apnea monitor, to detect decreased rates of breathing or heart beats.

If the child is on supplemental oxygen, environmental safety issues are of great importance, since oxygen is highly flammable. Early intervention personnel should verify that all electrical equipment is properly grounded and maintained, and certainly no one should smoke in the same room as the oxygen supply. In fact, second-hand smoke is an additional hazard, and should be strongly safeguarded against.

Apnea monitors have leads that frequently become disconnected during physical activity, triggering the alarm. Everyone involved with the child's recreational program should be instructed about how to check the child for signs and symptoms of apnea or bracycardia (and what appropriate action to take), how to check the leads and reconnect them if necessary, and how to turn off the alarm.

Hematologic Problems

Infants and toddlers with bleeding disorders such as hemophilia can be safely included in recreational activities as long as a few precautions are taken. These genetic disorders are caused by a deficiency in clotting factors that are necessary to stop bleeding and form a clot. In Factor VIII deficiency (or classic hemophilia), or Factor IX deficiency (Von Willibandts disease) injuries to the skin producing a laceration or trauma to the joints (which can cause internal bleeding) should be avoided if at all possible. Possible precautions include:

1. Review the recreational environment to identify any sharp edges, uneven surfaces, or areas where there is inadequate lighting that could increase the likelihood of a fall.

2. Avoid any "rough and tumble" play.
3. Consider protective devices, such as knee and elbow pads or protective helmets, depending upon the needs or the child and the potential for injury.

The risk of overprotection needs to be balanced against the very real possibility of significant bleeding and long-term sequellae of intra-joint bleeding.

The other more common but less obvious hematologic disorder that affects young children is anemia (or low red blood cell count). This can be secondary to an inherited disorder such as sickle cell anemia, due to an improper diet (such as iron deficiency anemia), or related to a toxic condition such as lead poisoning, where the lead interfers with the production of red blood cells, causing anemia, In all cases, a mildly low red blood count is frequently asymptomatic, but greater degrees of anemia are associated with fatigue, decreased energy, and irritability at times. Medical evaluation and treatment is essential, since many of these conditions are treatable. As it relates to recreational activities, the child's active participation should be evaluated based upon physical endurance and energy level, which may improve as the condition is treated. For children with sickle cell anemia, intermittent painful episodes (called "crises") may require a transition from active to passive participation until the episode has resolved.

Seizure disorders

Seizure disorders, or epilepsy, may take many forms, from brief loss of contact (called absence or partial seizures), to generalized major motor seizures, characterized by loss of conciousness and forceful shaking of the arms and legs. One type of seizure unique to infants is called "infantile spasms", where the young child may have repeated episodes of head drop and body flexion, generally occurring many times a day.

Most forms of seizure disorder are treated with anticonvulsant medication, which are usually taken several times a day.

Frequent side effects of this type of medication include lethargy, hyperactivity, or nausea. Some medications may produce photosensitivity, requiring the child to be protected from the sun. In addition, some specific seizure types are photosensitive, in that the seizures may be stimulated by light, particularly flickering light.

Three basic considerations impact upon the recreation program of a child with a seizure disorder. The first is determining whether there are any seizure triggers or medication side effects that must be avoided during recreation. The second is to determine whether any protections are needed for the child while participating in recreational activities, for example a protective helmet if frequent seizures are associated with sudden falls. The third concern is establishing a clear protocol for any action to be taken if a seizure occurs during the recreational activity. All of these concerns should be incorporated into the child's recreational plan in advance of its implementation.

Allergies

For most families, having a child who is allergic to a food or an environmental substance is a minor concern. However, some children have multiple or severe allergic reactions that can even become life threatening. It is important, therefore, to determine not only the presence of any specific allergies, but to determine how the allergic reaction is typically manifested (for example, does the child get a skin rash or have trouble breathing)?

In all cases, a plan should be developed to avoid exposure to the offending allergen (for example, having the parent provide snacks), and an emergency plan developed in advance if an allergic reaction should occur. This might include having emergency medication on hand but safely stored (such as an "epi pen"— an emergency dose of epinephrine), if the risk of severe allergic reaction is not totally avoidable. This might occur during outdoor activities for a child who is severely allergic to bee stings. Criteria should be established for when the emergency medication would be used, personnel trained in its administration, and a protocol developed for checking the medication on a regular basis. Latex allergies, in particular, can be potentially severe and should be recognized and an avoidance plan developed, and clear alternatives identified.

Chronic Infections

Infants and toddlers with chronic infections may be asymptomatic, and therefore even undiagnosed. For children with diagnosed chronic infections, such as cytomegalovirus (CMV), or herpes simplex virus (HSV) infections, the primary concern may be to prevent the spread of the infection to other children or staff. This is best accomplished by practicing universal precautions, including good hand washing.

For children with human immunodeficiency virus (HIV) infection, an additional concern is to prevent the child from being exposed unnecessarily to acute infections from other children or staff, since their immune system may be compromised and unable to adequately fight off infection. This can cause even simple infections to progress into much more serious or disseminated illness. Simple measures, such as universal precautions and especially good hand washing limits the spread of many infections. Parents should be informed that their children should not participate in a recreational activity if they have an acute illness, to prevent the spread to other children and staff. In addition, all toys and equipment should be properly cleaned between users to prevent the spread of infectious agents.

Summary

Infants and toddlers with developmental delays and with special health care needs should participate in recreational activities to promote social development. To accomplish this safely, it is advantageous for the early intervention team, which includes the family, to develop a recreation plan that identifies goals, strategies, precautions, and specific responses should problems arise. Information dissemination and appropriate training and special equipment should be identified and obtained, if needed. Varying degrees of active and passive participation may be necessary, depending upon the child's health status at the time of the activity. Including the child's physician in the planning is essential to incorporate all necessary health safeguards. This should enable all infants and toddlers with disabilities to participate effectively in appropriate recreational activities in a safe and health-promoting manner.

References

American Heritage Dictionary, (1982). Boston: Houghton. Rubin and Crocker (Eds.), Fulton and Goldhaber p. 230

CHAPTER 8
Development of Recreation and Leisure Through Art Interventions

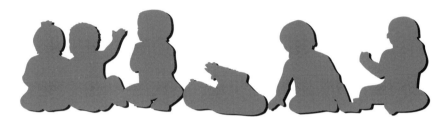

Valerie Smitheman-Brown

Most adults consider that play and art activities are naturally forming leisure skills for infants and toddlers. This chapter will ask the question: What are the true values of play and art activities for the infant and toddler? In examining the work of play and art, we will be charting the development of leisure and recreation skills.

A review of the actual processes of play and art and their accompanying activities will give us a snapshot of how leisure and social skills are extensions of the work of play. Play mirrors the growth of developing relationships, acts as a transitional object in the growth of object permanence, aides in the outpouring of emotional overflow, and spurs the exploration of the expanding imagination. In describing play and art activities for infants and toddlers, important non-verbal learning tools in the development of leisure and recreational skills are illustrated. In regard to art, this chapter will begin to investigate the development of visual representation skills through the use of pre-art materials as a means of stimulat-

ing important sensorimotor work, increasing communication of emotions, and the capacity to recognize tasks through various motor, signal, and symbolic meaning. The work of play and art will begin to take on a more significant aspect in the growth of infants and toddlers toward increasing their capability to respond to naturally occurring rejuvenation opportunities of leisure and recreation.

Theories of Play

There are a variety of theories of play, each focusing on the hypothesis of the researcher. A brief examination of the major assumptions indicates that while the proposed end results may appear different, play is a healthy and natural outlet and has a significant impact on the outcome of adult life. Cognitive developmental theorists such as Piaget (1955) have postulated that play and other environmental experiences create a link between the developing child's rational thinking and the outside world. Psychoanalytical theories described by Freud (1917) and Mahler (1975) look upon play as a useful form of mastery of anxiety increasing capacity for appropriate conflict resolution. Erikson's (1950,1968) social ideology speaks of play and art as expressions of social cognition, perspective, and peer relationships. Winnicott (1971) considers play a necessary element in the development of a differentiation between objects or persons. He reasons that play represents the practice of individuation from a symbiotic relationship with mother into a more independent being. Each theoretical stance has substantial merit and each theory subscribes to the realization that, play is all work.

Categories of play

Parten (1932) developed an elaborate categorization of children's play. Through observation of children in pre-school settings, she emphasized the role of play in the social context. Parten's observations describe a type of play that is considered heavily based on relationship activity. Her observations and categorization are generally accepted as continuing to be an accurate description in contemporary society. A short summary of these divisions will be helpful in exploring play activities.

- *Unoccupied play:* Occurs when a child is engaged in a non-goal-oriented activity, such as looking around leisurely.
- *Solitary play:* Playing alone, engrossed in their own activities without requiring or paying attention to others.
- *Onlooker play:* Occurs when a child watches other children play without entering into the activity.
- *Parallel play:* When a child plays separately but in tandem with others in a manner that might be described as imitative.
- *Associative play:* Play that involves social interaction with little or no organization, such as leading a line, exchanging toys, etc.
- *Cooperative play:* Involving social interaction in a group within an organized activity.

More recently, Bergin (1988) has developed a theory that emphasizes the cognitive aspect of play. His descriptions include sensorimotor and practice play, pretense/symbolic play, social play, constructive play, and games. In these cognitive divisions, the exploration accentuates play as a systematic learning experience.

- *Sensorimotor play:* Engaging in behavior that derives pleasure from motor experiences.
- *Practice play:* Involves the perseveration of a behavior focusing on learning new skills in which physical or mental mastery and coordination of skills is required.
- *Pretense/symbolic play:* This play denotes a higher skill when object permanence has been established and a child can relate a concrete object into a symbolic form.
- *Social play:* Involves interaction with a peer or group of peers.

Play Processes and Activities

In describing play and art processes and activities for infants and toddlers, we are illustrating valuable non-verbal learning tools in the development of leisure and recreational skills. The social and cognitive categories of play that were described in the previous section are useful tools with which to examine the actual processes.

Processes

Process is the act of doing, the manner of being active rather than a passive participant in the surroundings. In the development of infant and toddler play, there are several recognized stages of growth: solitary play, parallel play, modeling, imitation, and socialization. In observing infants and toddlers engaging in play, we can detect continuous, overlapping growth of both social and cognitive skills.

- *Solitary play*: The earliest stage of exploration of the infant and his environment must be a solitary endeavor. Until birth the infant had been an integral part of the mother and had developed a truly symbiotic relationship. Being alone is a new skill that must be acquired. Post birth, the stage of individuation can be described as the cognitive understanding of the "what is me/what is not me". This first individuation entails the knowledge of where we leave off and the environment begins. Being able to play in isolation is an important expansion of the self.

- *Parallel Play:* This term describes play characterized by playing side by side. While children appear to be playing together, the children are engaging in play focused on each of their own activities. Children may acknowledge each other and make eye contact during this period.

- *Imitation & Modeling:* This term explains the aspect of play that is a mirroring of the learning experience. It is very much like a try-out period. Infants observe others and tentatively duplicate the actions they see in their attempt to play. Imitation involves attention, retention, motor reproduction, and incentive conditions. Imitation is a learning skill that we can use throughout our lives from the infant process of imitating facial expressions to learning to kick a ball through observation. Modeling is a style of imitation that involves interaction with another usually the parent or caregiver, such as clapping hands or playing patty-cake.

- *Socialized play:* Playing with others is a reciprocal, bi-directional socialization. The parent-child aspect of socializing begins with the non-verbal interactions of motor movement. The parent and caregiver role in socialization is to scaffold a framework around which they and their infants can interact. The prime focus of scaffolding is the introduction of social rules to children.

Infant-parent games involve turn taking and sequencing opportunities. Games such as peek-a-boo are examples of turn taking. Socialized play begins the process of attachment. In his discussions, Erikson (1968) postulates that the first year of life represents the stage of trust versus mistrust. Trust requires a feeling of physical comfort and a minimal amount of fear and apprehension. Trust sets the stage for lifelong expectations of freedom, sensitivity, and love. Trust is a basic requirement for team sports and game playing.

As the infant matures into toddlerhood, social play begins to extend to other children. Exposure to peers gives the child an opportunity to practice social rules, to put into place the models learned from the parent. Social play also allows the child to practice the trust learned from the parent. Socialized play involves the rules that society has dictated as acceptable. A toddler must learn how to follow the social rules in play in order to comprehend the more complex rules of games and sporting activities.

Activities

When an infant is alone in her crib or stroller engaging in movement of hands and feet, swatting the air, attempting to follow a form or color with her eyes, she is engaging in sensorimotor play. Through observation we can assume that there is pleasure simply through the act of the motor experiences. Reacting reflexively, responding to auditory and visual stimuli, and random touching are examples of sensory experiences. By stimulating the senses through specific motor play activities, the infant begins the learning processes.

Infants enjoy making things work, having objects perform in a consistent manner in response to their actions. Toys that hang safely in the crib in a predictable place are objects that can be acted upon. A touch produces a consequence, an early exploration of cause and effect. A playful touch is a manipulation of the environment equaling a sense of control. In reaching for a toy, a finger, a foot, or even the side of the crib, the infant is investigating the boundaries of his world. What is the feel of playfully kicking your feet in the air and having the atmosphere around you respond? Perhaps it is the pleasure of movement alone that stimulates the joyful response. Movement in play allows for the practicing the control of bodily functions and is a precursor of the increasingly more complex tasks such as crawling and walking, pushing and throwing, and kicking and jumping. In gaining control of body movement in a cause and effect manner the infant is preparing for future physical leisure and recreational activities requiring gross motor skills.

There have been numerous studies on infant eye movement documenting the stabilization of the process of seeing. Swatting an object with hands and/or feet creates a movement of the object and the visual exploration of that movement. In the process of playing, the infant is utilizing and strengthening his visual acuity and the ability to observe objects in motion. In engineering the play area it is advantageous to display objects from right to left in order to encourage eventual reading skills through sight orientation.

It has long been held that bright colors will catch the infant's eye. Colors and simple shapes are a major influence in all of our lives and are used most effectively in infant and toddler toys when presented in a coordinated, orderly fashion for play. It is not difficult to overload the visual and emotional fields with vivid color. Introductions of colors through play and art materials should be slow and systematic. By presenting a color through the integration of multiple senses, such as sight, touch, and taste, we systematically introduce an understanding of color in play through the cognitive processes. The color red could be introduced through an appropriately sized red ball to stimulate sight and touch, strained red beets or strawberries to stimulate taste and smell, and red socks on the infant's feet for a more personal visual effect. The activities noted above open the sensory receptors to several levels of the perception of the color.

By approximately nine months of age, the infant begins to select toys of particular interest and toys that are novel. They enjoy acting upon toys and playing with objects that react to them. By their first birthday, infants are beginning to work more deliberately with objects exploring cause and effect in a serious manner. Toys that talk, play music, or move continue to stimulate the sensory receptors in a progressively mature manner. This type of play can be solitary play or in conjunction with others in a parallel situation.

As new skills are being learned in the areas of physical and motor mastery/coordination, the process of practice play is put into motion. Practice play is a lifetime skill, contributing to the continuing development of coordinated motor skills that are needed for sports and general game playing. Running, jumping, sliding, and throwing, are examples of practice play. These activities are engaged in on various levels of personal maturity. The toddler who is learning to jump over a stick on the ground is practicing as important a skill as the Olympic high-jump specialist who is trying to attain a clean jump over a seven-foot bar. Practice play can be a solitary or a group activity.

When a toddler begins to employ objects as tools in pretend play, they have achieved object constancy and are venturing into symbolism. Substitution of one object for another requires a more sophisticated cognitive mechanism requiring the ability to initiate transformation and individuate. This type of pretend/symbolic play can appear around 18-20 months and continues through pre-school years. Children with the ability to use objects as substitution or props are displaying an increasingly mature development of imaginative skills. Most pretend play involves themes, plots, and role-playing. The popular role of superhero is a prime example of pretend/symbolic play. Superheroes are richly endowed with superhuman powers. In the process of this pretend activity the toddler is able to expand his world, solve his problems, control the environment, and receive praise and recognition all with the speed of light. In a world dominated by adults this type of play allows a child to take on the power role in a practice situation.

As with all levels of maturity, increased guidance is necessary to assist the child in an appropriate direction. With the appearance of pretend/symbolic play, parents can act as a coach to assist in framing constructive and appropriate play experiences. It is important for the infant and toddler to understand the boundaries between pretend and real situations. Setting clear boundaries on pretend/symbolic play and clarifying the inappropriateness of violence or aggression in play are duties of the parents and caregivers. What is playing? What is pretend? These are areas that are often assumed but actually need to be taught in order to keep the toddler safe. Pretend/symbolic play is often done in parallel with others and is the beginning of socialization with peers.

Pretend/symbolic play normally involves some level of theme and role-playing. A narrative or story approach is an excellent intervention for parents to set boundaries for play and increase socialization skills. Landa (1998) describes a narrative or story as a window to social cognition, pragmatics, and language. Narratives make use of the rules of social interaction and provide an organized framework for the child. Narratives and stories are easily individualized to reach the level of representation, language complexity, and social competence of the child.

The process of social play involves social interaction with peers. This can be accomplished on several levels: onlooker, parallel, associative, and cooperative play. This type of play can be broken up into developmental and social cognition. The onlooker is a child who watches others play without entering into the activity. At a young age this is a very valuable learning experience. By observation, the toddler is cognitively processing the movements and attitudes of the children he is watching. He will attempt to assimilate that play culture into his own actions and reactions. As a toddler becomes more confident he may move

to the edge of the circle of peers and play in tandem, utilizing imitative or mirroring process in a practice mode.

When a toddler begins to join a line, ride down the slide with others, share a toy, or pass a book to another child, he is beginning to interact spontaneously. In associative play there is little or no organization to the activity. The toleration of close proximity is the main goal of the activity.

Constructive play and social play involve joining peers in organized sharing and interaction. Building a puzzle or constructing Lego's with another child is a form of constructive play. This type of social play requires that the toddler be able to tolerate another peer in a sharing activity.

As each level of play overlaps and then develops, the infant and toddler is growing toward solidifying skills that they will use in future leisure and recreation activities. It can be hypothesized that the child's level of maturity to engage in play activities will be a determining factor in the type of adult activities he may prefer. A child who has never become comfortable with organized games or is awkward with peer interaction may chose a more solitary sport to engage in as an adult; for example, he may prefer golf to baseball.

Relationships and Play

Throughout life, relationships are a delicate balance between individuals. In infancy relationships develop on a sensory level with adults and caretakers facilitating as the arouser, the satisfier, and the provider of basic needs. Relationship strategies during the earliest stages of play include body contact and touch; physical interventions; structure and consistent routine; caring and stimulation. Play during this period should consist of enticing rather than demanding reciprocation; stimulating sensory activities; and consistent, predictable routines. Establishment of a rudimentary sense of trust opens the opportunity for eventual mutuality.

As the infant matures to toddlerhood, the adult remains the predictable point of reference but the roles change from stimulator to motivator; from sole provider to boundary protector and supporter. Environmental elements should allow for safe and structured exploration, increased communication opportunities, frequent physical and verbal contact, and a reflection of action, feelings, and success.

It is at the point of the development of social play that peers become an important element of everyday life. This is when capacity for social play and imagination increases dramatically. Play encourages additional exploration, increases affiliation with peers, and provides an opportunity to examine areas of relationships that are more challenging. A sense of autonomy is beginning to develop as the child takes more risks in relationships.

Creative Arts in Leisure and Recreation Skills

It is said that drawing is a natural pastime for most children and from all indications reflects the ability of the child to make a mark on the world. From tiny beginnings there is evidence that drawing becomes a narrative of understanding the environment and our position within those surroundings. By encouraging creative art and drawing skills with even the youngest of children we are offering an alternative method of communication and self-expression. Lofty learning tools aside, creative arts and drawing are unique, pleasurable experiences that directly and indirectly have the effect of developing independent leisure and recreation skills.

Pre-art/Sensorimotor Work

Pre-art/sensorimotor work is a period when kinesthetic movement is encouraged for the sake of pleasure alone. As discussed earlier in this chapter, an infant appears to achieve a sense of delight and satisfaction from the simple movement of his hands and feet in the air. There is an environmental response that produces a valuable reciprocal interaction. The kinesthetic and tactile input an infant receives yields important information on cause and effect, on the ability to control his environment through his actions. By six months of age the infant is sitting and experiencing a wider view of the world. He has realized that his motor actions will produce the desirable effect. Even though all the senses are not cognitively integrated, there is some sense of mastery of gross motor movement.

Considering the importance of encouragement of sensory integration to heighten the learning processes, pre-art materials are a useful tool for exploration and expression. These kinesthetic explorations involve motor movement, such as actions and gestures, which can include rubbing, turning, scratching, and pulling. On the sensory level, pre-art takes on exploration predominantly through touch and haptic sense. Touch provides a feedback about surface qualities. Weight, shape, and texture of an object or material are experienced. Sensory experiences of external objects also enhance imagery formation. Vivid sensory experiences lead to more vivid memory.

The kinesthetic/sensory level activity extends infants the opportunity to let go of inhibitions and control. Interaction with the materials can lead to an awareness of the rhythm created through the integrated action of cause and effect.

What is pre-art? Pre-art involves practicing our unique creativity with materials that are commonplace and can be integrated into the sensorimotor level. Exploration with pre-art materials includes construction, drawing, sculpting, and collage. Encounters with pre-art materials are fun. The most common materials are food items, liquid items, fabrics, textiles, sponges, pieces of paper, and large plastic pieces.

How many have not observed a small child play with his food? This is considered a spontaneous and solitary exploration and is probably not a good social skill to encourage. We can, however, offer these kinesthetic and tactile experiences in more controlled situations as interactive play.

Food is a particularly good exploratory pre-art material in that it is non-toxic and has a variety of textures. With sensorimotor pre-art work with food it is suggested that a specific art tray with 1″ sides be used to contain messiness and offer a concrete area for the child to associate with art.

- *Pudding play:* Pudding imitates the consistency of finger paint. Place room temperature pudding on the art tray. Join with the infant in creating designs in the pudding. This activity will advocate experience while it indirectly nourishes control through modeling. Valuable input in motor control, control of design, and tactile information can be obtained through pudding play.

- *Oatmeal sand:* Oatmeal has several attributes that make it ideal construction materials. Oatmeal can be moved around, sifted, piled into cups and bowls, and if you add water you can mound it like a sandcastle.

- *Spice collage:* Apply beaten egg whites in random patterns on the tray. Introduce a variety of spices for the child to finger and apply to the egg white. The spices will adhere to the egg whites. This activity also encourages olfactory distinctions.

- *Mashed potato mountains:* Mashed potatoes have a thicker consistency and entice building. They can be mounded, pulled, sculpted, smashed, and then re-mounded. For the young child who has not yet shown an ability to apply distinctions, some food coloring in the potatoes will assist in reinforcing the art concept to the work.

- *Marshmallow tower:* Provide large marshmallows and pretzel sticks to encourage stacking and building skills for future incorporation into creating.

- *Touch bags:* Introduction of a variety of tactile experiences increases the ability to distinguish through the sense of feel. Pre-art materials that have tactile properties will need to have more supervision, as they are not always safe for oral experiences. Sew a variety of 5″ cotton bags. In each bag place materials that will identify different tactile experiences.

Soft: Fill bag with cotton balls
Hard: Fill bag with coffee beans
Fuzzy: Outside of the bag should be velour
Smooth: Outside of the bag should be satinlike

- *Sponge painting:* With a household sponge as a tool, encourage the child to dip, drip, press, smear, and create with jelly on the art tray. This activity increases fine motor control and allows the child to experience distinct designs.

- *Jell-O jiggles:* Jell-O is a fascinating food material. It can be wiggly, gushy, smooth, and is bright colored. By using large blocks of Jell-O or small shapes of Jell-O the child can explore the slipperiness of the material, work on fine motor control, and have fun watching the reaction of the material to touch.

These are a few pre-art materials that can be safely used to encourage creativity, exploration, and discovery of leisure skills though everyday materials. By utilizing these suggestions as a jumping-off point, many different tactile and kinesthetic experiences can be presented to the infant that will expand his knowledge of what brings joy, excitement, and expression.

Scribble Stage of Representation

Grasping a crayon and making a mark is a deceptively simple and natural task, but should be considered an important developmental milestone. Early attempts at scribbling can be considered the first indication of self-expression, and while it may appear disordered and random, recent research reports that there is a pattern of growth to be observed and discovered that is unique to each child.

The initial marks made by a child are basically kinesthetic in nature. Although early scribbling cannot be considered a purposeful attempt to portray a personal view of the visual environment, the unconditional acceptance of these first attempts encourages drawing as an acceptable avenue for leisure, recreation, and communication activities.

Each at his own pace, children begin to understand that there is a definite connection between the kinesthetic movement of their arms and hands and the marks that they are making on paper. They begin to attempt to have some control over the markings. This discovery often reflects the level of control the child is gaining in other areas of her environment.

Most adults would say that they could recognize a scribble when they saw one and are dismissive of the labor. However, much like a child's first utterances, beginning scribbles are a benchmark. Lowenfeld (1952) and Lowenfeld & Brittain (1987) describe scribbling as the first permanent record of a child's existence. For an understanding of young children, it is important that scribbling be recognized as part of the total growth pattern. Most children pursue scribbling vigorously and explore their environment through a variety of senses. Some of these experiences are reflected in their scribbles. The drawings have a healthy variety, beginning with random markings, changing to continuous or controlled motions and becoming more complex when labeling begins.

This period of life is an important stage for developing self-assurance and observing the environment. The record left by the child when he scribbles is an individual chronicle of his perception of his world. During the scribble period, the role of parent in encouraging growth in self-expression through art experiences is very important. Providing stimulation, encouragement, and the motivation necessary for developing an increased awareness of internal and external experiences is a prime duty.

Research shows that scribbles tend to follow a fairly predictable order. They begin with random marks on a paper and evolve into recognizable representations.

Disordered scribbles vary in length and direction. There may be some repetition of marks due to the rhythmic motion of the arms. Often eye contact will not be necessary to continue to draw. An important element of the disordered scribble is to recognize that the child is not portraying elements in the visual environment, but rather a fascination with the ability to control and create marks. Even at this early stage, scribbling should be nourished through verbal and non-verbal praise.

Controlled scribbling indicates that there is a level of direction expressed in the work. A child has discovered that there is a connection between her motions and the marks on the paper. When they discover this coordination between visual and motor activity, children are usually motivated to vary their motions. The evolution of a more deliberate scribbling effort offers us the opportunity to detect practicing experiences. Specific skills can be observed as body image is developing, hand preferences are emerging, and real integration of visual and motor apparatus is beginning. Overriding the developmental milestones is the pure enjoyment experienced through kinesthetic sensation and the ability to control marks.

As scribbling becomes more purposeful and labeling begins to occur, (verbally or non-verbally) doors to imagination open wide. Being mindful to exhibit unconditional acceptance of the child's personal metarepresentational image, the avenue of coordinating labeled scribbling with narrative discourse through storytelling will advance interactive communication. In working with narratives, a substantial effort should be made to attend to the child's intentions of drawing, referencing, and any presuppositions that are attempted when expressing through artwork. At this phase, images may take on several labels as the narrative advances, so flexibility is a required virtue in order to continually encourage the communicative connection of the artwork and the child's mental model of his relationship with the world.

Integral to the process of observation and joining with the child in the act of scribbling is the aspect of socialization. Sitting with the child, showing interest, scribbling and modeling the child's work, commenting on the art, sharing the space, etc., are all excellent exercises in socialization. This is a chance to interact nonverbally and model social cues through body language that are crucial to beginning to address social cognition. This primarily non-verbal interaction allows a child to gradually work through isolative tendencies in an anxiety-reducing and non-threatening shared space. Parallel modeling of the drawing is a concrete nonverbal signal of acceptance of any child's approximations of imagery.

Materials

Suggestions for drawing materials to proffer a toddler are media that extend a measure of control. Squared-off crayons, bulky pencils, and large pieces of chalk are easily grasped and make substantial marks. Plain white or colored paper is preferable to any coloring books or drawings that require working within pre-drawn shapes. At this point of development, toddlers are not able to contain within lines and this activity can cause frustration. Additional creative materials suggested are pre-formed wood pieces, cutouts, and soft clay for construction work.

Summary

Play and art are work. Erect a sign: DEVELOPMENT IN PROGRESS. Activities that appear to be simple pleasurable experiences are, in fact, complex developmental milestones in the evolution of leisure and recreation skills.

In the process of learning, the child's interaction with the environment is crucial. During the sensory level of processing, motor activity is a vital pathway to expansion of the capacity to regulate hand/eye activities for future sports and game action. Information received from concrete, kinesthetic work is assimilated in a manner that answers the sensory, pleasure, and learning processes.

In the area of cognition, the scribble stage of visual development coincides with Piaget's description of infant behavior as primarily sensorimotor. Children in the scribble phase are practicing skills in sequencing, observation, structural organization, balance, generalization, discrimination of details, and advanced fine motor coordination. The above are requirements for the progression of self-expression and choice in reading, written skills, visual arts, and performing arts.

References

Bergin, D. (1988). Stages of play development. In D. Bergin (Ed.), *Play as a medium for learning and development.* Portsmouth, N.H.: Heineman.

Erikson, E. (1950). *Childhood and society.* N.Y.: W.W. Norton.

Erikson, E. (1968). *Identify: Youth in crisis.* N.Y.: W.W. Norton.

Freud, S., (1917). *A general introduction to psychoanalysis.* N.Y.: Washington Square Publishers.

Landa, R. (1998). *What's in a story? A narrative approach to social interaction.* Presentation: 1st Conference on Autism, Baltimore, MD.

Lowenfeld, V. (1952). *The nature of creative activity.* (Rev. Ed) N.Y.: Harcourt Publishing.

Lowenfeld, V., & Brittain, W.L. (1987). *Creative and mental growth.* (8th Ed.). N.Y.: Macmillian Publishing.

Mahler, M. (1975). *The psychological birth of the human infant.* N.Y.: Hutchinson.

Piaget, J. (1955). *The language and thought of the child.* N.Y.: Meridian.

Parten, M. (1932). "Social play among pre-school children." *Journal of Abnormal and Social Psychology, 27,* 243-269

Santrock, J., & Yussan, S. (1992). *Child development.* IA: Wm. C. Brown Publishers.

Winnicott, D.W. (1971). *Playing and reality.* London: Tavistock Publishing Limited.

Appendices

Appendix A

VACATION

Leisure in the Summer for the Young Child

- Visit the park with an picnic lunch.

- Go to the library for an afternoon of children's books; bring home a child's educational video.

- Sign up for a recreation and parks program; coach a pre-school team.

- Check for a specialized day-camp offering therapeutic and recreational programs.

- Call your closest fitness club and check for community swim programs.

- Go to the art museum and explore the children's wing touch and see area.

- Collect recyclables and take them to the recycling center; donate the money to a favorite charity.

- Check with the YMCA for summer arts and crafts programs.

- Hire a college student to spend a couple of days a week doing planned and spontaneous activities.

- Plan a treasure hunt around the backyard or a neighborhood park.

- Buy a child's cook book and plan kids' cooking day.

Appendix B

Resources for Young Children

National Association for the Education of Young Children (NAEYC)
1509 16th St., NW
Washington, D.C. 20036-1426
Phone: (800) 424-2460 or locally (202) 232-8777
Fax: (202) 328-1846
http://www.naeyc.org/

The Council for Exceptional Children
Division for Early Childhood
1920 Association Drive, Reston, VA 20191-1589
Toll-free: 1-888-CEC-SPED | Local 703-620-3660
TTY (text only) 703-264-9446 | Fax 703-264-9494
http://dec-sped.org/

Autism Society of America
7910 Woodmont Avenue, Suite 300
Bethesda, MD 20814
1-800-3-autism
www.autism-society.org

NICHCY
National Information Center for Children and Youth with Disabilities
P. O. Box 1492
Washington, D.C. 20013
1-800-695-0285
email: nichcy@aed.org
www.nichcy.org

Family Resource Center on Disabilities
20 East Jackson Boulevard, Room 900
Chicago, IL 60604
1-800-332-2372

Head Start Bureau
Administration on Children, Youth and Families
U. S. Department of Health & Human Services
P. O. Box 1182
Washington, D.C. 20013
www.acf.dhhs.gov/programs/hsb

National Parent Network on Disabilities
1130 17th Street N.W., Suite 400
Washington, D.C. 20036
202-463-2299
email: npnd@cs.com
www.npnd.org

Special Olympics International
1325 G. Street N. W., Suite 500
Washington, D.C. 20005
202-628-3630
email: specialolympics@msn.com
www.specialolympics.org/

Early Intervention Related Links

Compiled by George Jesien, Ph.D.
http://dec-sped.org/eilinks.html

Exceptional Parent Magazine
555 Kinderkamack Road
Oradell, NJ 07649
(201) 634-6550
http://www.eparent.com/

KAPLAN
P. O. Box 609
1310 Lewisville-Clemmons Road
Lewisville, NC 27023-0609

(800) 334-2014
http://www.Kaplanco.com/

CLASSROMM Direct.com
P. O. Box 830677
Birmingham, AL 35283-0677
(800) 248-9171
http://www.classroomdirect.com/

Resources related to health and well being

Davidson, J. (1999). *The complete idiot's guide to managing stress* (2nd ed.). New York: Alpha Books.

Haas, E. M. (1981). *Staying healthy with the seasons.* Berkeley, CA: Celestial Arts.

Magaziner, A. (1999). *The complete idiot's guide to living longer and healthier.* New York: Alpha Books.

Resources related to brain development and children

Healy, J. M. (1994). *Your child's growing mind: A practical guide to brain development and learning from birth to adolescence.* New York: Doubleday.

Howard, P. J. (1994). *The owner's manual for the brain: Everyday applications from mind-brain research.* Austin, TX: Bard Press.

Sousa, D. R. (1995). *How the brain learns.* Reston, VA: National Association of Secondary School Principals.

Sylwester, R. (1995). *A celebration of neurons: An educator's guide to the brain.* Alexandria, VA: Association for Supervision and Curriculum Development.

Early Childhood Developmental Assessments

♦ *Temperament and Atypical Behavior Scale (TABS)*

Early Childhood Indicators of Developmental Dysfunction
by Stephen J. Bagnator, Ed.D., N.C.S.P., John T. Neisworth, Ph.D., John Salvia, D. Ed., & Frances M. Hunt, Ph.D.
Paul H. Brookes Publishing
P.O. 10624
Baltimore, MD 21285-0624
1-800-638-3775
www.brookespublishing.com

♦ *Assessment, Evaluation, and Programming System (AEPS) for Infants and Children*

Curriculum-based assessment and evaluation system
Paul H. Brookes Publishing
P.O. 10624
Baltimore, MD 21285-0624
1-800-638-3775
www.brookespublishing.com

♦ *Read, Play, and Learn*

Storybook Activities for Young Children
by Toni W. Linder, Ed.D.
Paul H. Brookes Publishing
P.O. 10624
Baltimore, MD 21285-0624
1-800-638-3775
www.brookespublishing.com

♦ *Developmental Assessment of Young
  Children*

by Judith K. Coress & Taddy Maddox
Identifies possible delays in the domains
of cognition, communication, social-
emotional development, physical development, and adaptive behavior.
pro-ed
8700 Shoal Creek Blvd.
Austin, Texas 78757-6897
1-800-897-3202
www.proedinc.com

♦ *Birth to Three Assessment and
  Intervention System*

Screening Test of Developmental Abilities
Comprehensive Test of Developmental
Abilities and Manual for Teaching Developmental Abilities
by Jerome J. Ammer & Tina Bangs
pro-ed
8700 Shoal Creek Blvd.
Austin, Texas 78757-6897
1-800-897-3202
www.proedinc.com

♦ *Peabody Development Motor Scales*

by M. Rhonda Folio & Rebecca R. Fewell
Designed to assess the motor skills of
children from birth through five years of
age.
pro-ed
8700 Shoal Creek Blvd.
Austin, Texas 78757-6897
1-800-897-3202
www.proedinc.com

Appendix C

Leisure Activities for Professionals and Families

Designed by Ginny Popiolek

The following activities can be implemented by professionals and families to support recreation and leisure using materials and settings that are typical in the everyday environment.

Activity: Catch with a Friend

Equipment: Elastic, beach ball, masking or electrical tape, Styrofoam peanuts.

Description: Cut a beach ball open about four inches and fill with the Styrofoam peanuts. Cover the opening with tape and attach the elastic to the valve at the end. Suspend the ball in front of the children. (you can add noise by using bells or change the weight by using shredded paper).

Motor: The child can be positioned in a sitting, kneeling, or sidelie position—whatever they are working on or prefer. Encourage the child to push the ball to her sibling or friend and catch it when it comes back. The ball will not hurt them if they don't catch it and they love the way it moves and sounds!

Language: The child can be encourage to say or gesture—"ball", "push", "more", "catch", and "my turn" along with any other language which pragmatically occurs.

Social: The child has an opportunity to play with a friend or sibling. It encourages eye contact and cooperative play at a low comfortable level.

Adaptions: If the child is ready for striking skills, this suspended ball is great for batting using their hand or a light plastic bat.

The children should be encouraged to take turns and to be a safe distance away from the batter.

Activity: Parachute

Equipment: Colorful flat sheet, family members or friend, light ball or beach ball.

Description: Spread the flat sheet on the floor and have individuals sit around the sheet. Each person should hold onto the sheet with both hands and shake it up and down. If your child is having difficulty holding on, you could have him sit between your legs and place your hand over his in a hand-over-hand method. (Also refer to adapted equipment at the end).

Try the following:

- Arms up-"peek-a-boo"-arms should stretch up and individuals are now seeing each other under the sheet.
- Arms up and down slowly—make waves.
- Arms up and down quickly to the floor and hold it. The sheet will make a mountain.
- Arms up and call one child's name and have him crawl or move to you.
- Arms up and place the child under the sheet and shake the sheet slowly above him.
- Place beach ball on the sheet and shake moving the ball around.
- With the ball on the sheet moves arms up and down and the ball will pop off.

Motor: This activity is wonderful for developing upper body strength, grasp, range of movement, trunk stability, visual tracking, and sensory integration.

Language: The following words or gestures, language, and concept development can be experienced and encouraged: "up", "down", "shake", "slow", "fast", "come", "name", "recognition", "off", "on".

Social: This activity promotes and provides experiences with following directions, name recognition, cooperative play, and taking turns.

Adaptations:

• These activities can be performed in various postures; tall kneeling, standing, sitting, etc. The Velcro sock can assist with experiencing and developing grasp when used with a handle sewn onto the sheet.

Velcro Sock drawing
Place the sock on the child's hand with fingers around the loop. The Velcro will close the grasp and assist children with tactile defensiveness or those who have not developed a grasp.

Activity: Row, Row, Row, Your Boat

Equipment: Towel, a partner.

Description: Adult and child are facing one another (two children can be used with an adult supervising). Various positions can be used: one person behind the child to assist with transfer to the floor and child's legs are crossed in front in a sitting position, same position but with no guarding, and the distance can be increased between the two people as the child gets stronger.

Adult and child hold hands and sing "row, row, row your boat" alternating sitting and lying down. A towel is used to hold onto as the child is ready for more difficulty. If using the towel, the child should demonstrate good head control—chin to chest.

Motor: This activity encourages good head control, abdominal and upper body strength, and hand grasp.

Language: This activity uses singing which assists with timing as well as imitating words and an opportunity to localize with music.

Social: This partner activity works on cooperative play and eye contact.

Activity: Prone Push

Equipment: Small, bright six inch ball, family and friends.

Description: Everyone is on the floor on their stomachs in a circle. The ball is pushed to other people in the circle using your hands. The group can encourage each other to move the ball quickly or slowly. If you miss and the ball goes out of the circle, you go get the ball. It is important to do this on a smooth surface in order for the ball to move. The group can decide to add more balls to increase the stimulation.

Motor: This activity encourages upper body strength, rotation and weight transfer, full range of movement, and visual tracking. This prone position is excellent for developing upper body stability and strength which is typically very weak and difficult to motivate children to improve.

Language: Words such as; "look", "push", "your turn", "fast", and "slow" can be use to increase vocabulary and concept development. Children can be encouraged to vocalize and request the ball as well as call other people's names.

Social: This activity requires turn-taking, eye contact, and waiting.

Adaptations: A sticker or mark can be placed on the ball to assist with tracking skills. Additional balls can be used, but it is recommended that no more than three be added, due to over stimulation. The child cannot focus on that much activity.

Activity: Walk the Path

Equipment: Bubble wrap, carpet samples cut length-wise in half.

Description: This activity may be set-up in various ways depending on the child's needs:

1. If the child is beginning to walk or has a wide gait, use the strips of carpet to form a path on both sides. Bubble wrap may be placed on top of the carpet. The child would then have an auditory and tactile reminder if they stepped "off the path".

2. The carpet may be used to form a line or path for the child to walk on. Bubble wrap can be placed on the side of the carpet. If they step off the path they would have tactile and sensory feedback to recognize that they are "off the path". This is a higher skill. Please be sure that the child is not afraid of the bubble wrap. Do not use if they are adverse to the bubble wrap.

Motor: This activity provides experience with weight-shifting, dynamic balance, kinesthetic awareness, and following visual cues.

Language: Concepts are developed related to on, off, walk, line, stop, start, as well as opportunities to articulate these concepts.

Social: This activity provides an opportunity to following auditory and visual directions as well as take turns.

Adaptations: If the child needs a motivator, use chips or tokens at one end and a jar or stacker at the other for the child to put them into.

Activity: Sponge Throw

Equipment: Sponges, water pail, sidewalk chalk.

Description: A design is made on the sidewalk using the sidewalk chalk. This design can be made by the child, sibling, friend, or parent. A pail is filled with water and sponges (cut to the appropriate size for their hands), and placed at a distance the child can throw. Child takes the sponge from the water and is encourage to squeeze sponge (assistance can be provided in a hand over hand method if needed). The child throws at the picture. As the sponge hits the picture, the water washes part of it away. Encourage children to throw until the picture it is "all gone".

Motor: This activity assists in developing hand grasp and strength, balance, rotational movements, stoop and recover, transitional movements, and eye-hand coordination.

Language: Language can be reinforced for words such as; "pick-up", "squeeze", "throw", "all gone", and "your turn".

Social: This activity provides an opportunity for cooperative play.

Adaptations: Children can share one pail and throw at one picture or each can have their own depending on their affective ability. The target and distance should be modified to meet individual needs and challenges. A child can simply release or push the sponge for their turn.

Activity: Obstacle Course

Equipment: Household furniture, sheets, and pillows

Description: Using materials in the house, set-up an obstacle course for the child, friends, and siblings to move through. Use some of these ideas:

- couch and chair cushions to; roll, crawl, or walk on. Position cushions sideways to form a path.
- pillows: step over or jump over.
- chairs: move back to back with a space and place a sheet over to form a tunnel or use to walk around.
- coffee table: go under or around.
- telephone books to step on and off of, or to step over.

Always be concerned about safety—edge or shape corners and guard the child at all times. It is important to set this up in accordance to the child's ability. Have fun!

Motor: This activity provides opportunity to develop all locomotor skills—walk, roll, crawl, as well as balance and motor planning.

Language: Spatial concepts and language can be reinforced such as; "in", "out", "on", "off", "through", "under", "over", "around", and "between".

Social: Parallel play and opportunities for taking turns can be provided with this activity.

Activity: Dance to the Music

Equipment: Fun music, small plastic bottles, food coloring, and water.

Description: The small plastic bottles (water bottles, etc.) are filled with a small amount of water and food coloring is added. It is more fun when each bottle is a different color. Adults and children hold a water bottle in each hand or the child may just have one bottle and hold with two hands. The music is turned on and they play follow the leader:

• march in place and swing arms
• arms up, hands shaking
• arms down and swinging
• shake everything
• arms in and out
• bend arms and stretch
• swing arms and twist

Motor: This activity is wonderful for developing upper body strength, imitative skills, cardiovascular endurance, full range of movement, and rhythmic movements.

Language: Concept development and articulation of words such as: up, down, swing, shake, and bend can be developed.

Social: This activity provides cooperative play, following directions and imitative skills. This is a great activity for family fun—Family Aerobics!

Activity: Balls, Balls Everywhere

Equipment: Paper, masking tape, tube socks, small balls, empty boxes of various sizes.

Description: Each child will make a ball as part of the activity. A piece of paper is given to each child. According to their ability, the child will use one or both hands to squeeze the paper into a small ball. The adult will put masking tape around the ball several times. Child's hands will need to be washed due to ink from the paper. Each child will be given a tube sock and place another ball in the sock. With the ball in the toe of the sock, a single knot will be made with the tube leaving a "tail and a ball". The boxes will be placed at various distances with children encouraged to throw the balls in the boxes.

Motor: This activity provides a wonderful opportunity for the child to feel the difference in the weight of the balls—sensory awareness, as well as grasp, and eye-hand coordination.

Language: Concepts and language develop with words such as "throw", "in", "heavy", "light", and "all done" can be experienced.

Social: Parallel and cooperative play can be experienced with this activity.

Activity: Bubbles

Equipment: Cushion, ball, and bubbles.

Description: Bubbles are utilized for visual tracking, reaching, touching, balance, and tolerating positions. The adult should use positions that are appropriate to the child's motor ability. Bubbles should be blown in front of the child to encourage reaching. One can be "caught" on the wand to facilitate movements. Positions such as side lie, sitting—tailor, side or long legged, half kneel, lying over a ball and bearing weight, straddle sitting over a roll–pillow, positioned in any of the child's equipment.

Motor: This activity presents the opportunity to emphasize reaching, balance, weight shifting, tracking, and tolerating positioning.

Language: This activity provides the child an opportunity to ask for "more" and "done", as well as the words "pop" and "bubbles".

Social: This activity encourages eye contact and facial interactions as well as taking turns and waiting.

Index